Everyman's Poetry

*Everyman, I will go with thee,
and be thy guide*

What Sweeter Music

Poems on Music

Selected and edited by
DOUGLAS BROOKS-DAVIES

EVERYMAN
J. M. Dent · London

This edition first published by Everyman Paperbacks in 1999
Selection, introduction and other critical apparatus
© J. M. Dent 1999

J. M. Dent
Orion Publishing Group
Orion House
5 Upper St Martin's Lane
London WC2H 9EA

Typeset by Deltatype Ltd, Birkenhead, Merseyside
Printed in Great Britain by
The Guernsey Press Co. Ltd, Guernsey, C. I.

British Library Cataloguing-in-Publication
Data is available on request

ISBN 0 460 88203 1

For Stephen Cleobury

Contents

Note on the Editor

DOUGLAS BROOKS-DAVIES was born in Wimbledon in 1942 and educated at Merchant Taylors' School, Crosby, and Brasenose College, Oxford. He was Senior Lecturer in English Literature at the University of Manchester until 1993 and is now an Honorary Research Fellow there. His hobbies are gardening, singing and playing the oboe.

The founder editor of Manchester University Press's Literature in Context series, he has published widely on Renaissance, eighteenth- and nineteenth-century English literature. His books include *Number and Pattern in the Eighteenth-Century Novel* (Routledge, 1973), *The Mercurian Monarch* (Manchester U. P., 1983), *Pope's 'Dunciad' and the Queen of Night* (Manchester U.P., 1985), and *Oedipal Hamlet* (Macmillan, 1989). Among his editions are *Silver Poets of the Sixteenth Century* (Dent, 1992), *Spenser's 'Fairy Queen'* (Dent, 1996), *Spenser: Selected Shorter Poems* (Longman, 1995), L.P. Hartley's *The Go-Between* (Penguin, 1997), and Henry Fielding's *Tom Jones* and Charlotte Brontë's *Jane Eyre* (both Dent, 1998). His previous volumes for the Everyman Poetry Library are *Alexander Pope* (1996), *Robert Herrick* (1996), *Four Metaphysical Poets* (1997), *Jane Austen* (1998) and *Sweet Will Be the Flower: Poems on Gardens* (1999).

Introduction

If there is one thing above all that music has the power to achieve in us, it is a sense of wonder. Anciently, this wonder expressed itself in the belief that the universe was ordered so that the planets, as they revolved in their orbits, emitted musical notes of inexpressible beauty; and in the haunting myth of Orpheus, founder of poetry and music according to Greek tradition, whose voice and mastery of the lyre were so exquisite that he could make animals, trees and rocks move as he performed, and who had the power even to move the king of the underworld to restore his dead wife to him.

The revolving planets produce, of course, the music of the spheres, unheard by mortals either because we are distanced from it by sin or simply because our aural channels are too narrow to detect it. Nevertheless our response to earthly music is conditioned, it was believed by the Neoplatonists, by our soul's memory of the celestial music, which it heard as it journeyed through those same spheres, garnering a virtue from each as it passed on its way from heaven into the foetus. A typical statement is the following, from the *Commentary on the Dream of Scipio*, Book II, chapter iii, of the fifth-century AD grammarian, Macrobius:

> the dead are accompanied to their tombs with singing because the soul is returning to its origin in the sweetest music, that is, heaven; all living things, even barbarians, are captivated by music, because the soul brings to the body a memory of heavenly music; hence the origin of the fable of Orpheus attracting animals and Amphion drawing rocks, for their songs first enraptured barbaric and irrational peoples, or those who were immovable like rocks.

Thus the soul was attuned to harmony; and a related belief held that the body was actually proportioned according to the basic musical intervals. Here the discovery – attributed to Pythagoras – that musical pitch could be described mathematically in terms of proportion, or ratios, was fundamental. (By this is meant the fact that on any stringed instrument, for example, a string, fixed at each end, produces a certain note: when the length of the string is halved

– by placing a finger on it at the midway point – the note produced by each half is an octave higher than the note originally sounded. Thus the ratio of one part to the other which produces this interval of the octave is 2:1. Obviously, other ratios produce different notes in relation to the given note of the open string.)

The refinement of this belief, as of so many others, was left to the Renaissance Neoplatonists, so that by the beginning of the sixteenth century the assumption that the various parts of the body were harmonious because they were in musical relationship with each other was common (see Cowley, *Davideis*, 30-1n.). Along with the inherent musicality of the soul, it explained the degree to which man, reflecting the divine harmony, was made in God's image (Genesis 2) and was thus a microcosmic reflection of the macrocosm. The theoretical underpinning of the belief is the subject of the passage from Cowley's *Davideis* excerpted in the present anthology, as also the first stanza of Dryden's 'A Song for St Cecilia's Day, 1687'.

In addition, harmony in Platonic thought is the prerequisite of beauty, so that a well-proportioned body is at once beautiful and musical. Hence Campion's Song: 'Rose-cheeked Laura, come,/Sing thou smoothly with thy beauty's/Silent music'. Similarly, it ill behoves a musician – particularly a church musician – to be immoral, for his soul must be in accord with the music he professes. Thus George Wither, in 'For a Musician':

> What will he gain
> By touching well his lute,
> Who shall disdain
> A grave advice to hear?
> What from the sounds
> Of organ, fife or lute
> To him redounds
> Who doth no sin forbear?
> A mean respect
> By tuning strings he hath
> Who doth neglect
> A rectified path.

It is worth remarking, incidentally, that the English Reformation fostered a brilliant tradition of church music, and that this 'English Music' (to borrow the title of Peter Ackroyd's novel of 1992) fostered in turn a rich tradition of poetry about music, much of which I have drawn on here, including George Herbert's 'Easter' and 'Church Music' (where music 'know[s] the way to heaven's door'), Henry Vaughan's 'The Morning Watch' ('Prayer is/The world in tune'), and Milton's *Il Penseroso*, with its Cambridge chapel in which the music brings 'all heaven before' the poet narrator's eyes, thereby reminding us of music's power to induce ecstasy.

After all, if the soul is heaven-derived and contains within it the memory of the planetary music, then any beautiful music – instrumental or vocal – was regarded as having the theoretical potential to draw the soul back to its divine origins. The Platonist in Wordsworth could still feel this, also in Cambridge, as he attended Evensong in King's College Chapel (in the first of the two sonnets by him on the topic included in this anthology):

> that branching roof . . .
> Where light and shade repose, where music dwells
> Lingering – and wandering on as loath to die:
> Like thoughts whose very sweetness yieldeth proof
> That they were born for immortality.

A century later Sir Edmund Gosse could still write, in 'Unheard Music', of the 'dear sounds that soar and clamour at heaven's high gate . . . far above our octaves'.

As a matter of inevitability and not merely as empty compliment, the theme appears in the sub-genre of elegies on dead musicians, whether they be now-forgotten, like Anna Seward's beloved counter-tenor John Saville of Lichfield Cathedral choir ('But thy pure spirit fled from pains and fears/To sinless, changeless, everlasting spheres') or the still-celebrated, as in Dryden's 'Ode, on the Death of Mr Henry Purcell':

> We beg not hell our Orpheus to restore:
> Had he been there,
> Their sovereign fear
> Had sent him back before.
> The power of harmony too well they know:
> He long ere this had tuned their jarring sphere
> And left no hell below.

> The heavenly choir, who heard his notes from high,
>   Let down the scale of music from the sky:
>   They handed him along. . . .

The musician-as-Orpheus resolves the discords of hell and, through the power of the musical scale (from Latin *scala*, ladder) that he has mastered so thoroughly, earns his entry into heaven where he sings with angels (who were now regarded as custodians of the planetary music). Similarly, the poet T. E. Brown two centuries after Dryden visualises the great church musician Samuel Sebastian Wesley storming heaven at his death and being rewarded for his earthly devotion by the most splendid of celestial pipe organs on which he will play music finer than any heard in heaven.

Music stirs the soul, governs the heavenly spheres, can even conquer death. And, of course, Orpheus and others were regarded as being able to control animals and inanimate objects. Hence arose the poetic tradition of speculation on the relationship between the musical instrument, mute when laid aside by its owner but sounding gloriously when played by him or her, and its physical origin in mere inanimate wood, bamboo, or whatever: for example, William Drummond's 'Sonnet 8', and Shelley's 'With a Guitar, to Jane' and John Lyly on Pan's flute deriving from the reed into which Daphne was metamorphosed.

Above all, though, it is the voice that recurs as the predominant musical instrument, the thing that stirs us above anything else: the beloved singing rouses the lover's soul; our 'understanding voice' is overheard by the angels and somehow repairs, for a moment, the discord of sin (Milton, 'At a Solemn Music'); the lone girl sings of long ago and far away, melancholy and deeply moving (Wordsworth's 'The Solitary Reaper').

Whether Wordsworth knew of the long tradition, in Quintilian, St John Chrysostom, and others, of mentioning the strange power of the singing of the solitary labourer does not matter. What does matter is the way writers on music visit and revisit certain themes which lie, like an ostinato ground bass, infinitely repeating itself, while their words, like notes, 'vary, re-vary; tune and tune again' above it (I quote from Joshua Sylvester's hauntingly appropriate 'Variable', reprinted in this anthology).

This Introduction has deliberately emphasised the more esoteric aspects of the traditions on which many of my chosen poems dwell. This is not to deny the immediacy of many of the older poems, and certainly not to make them formidable. It is rather, alongside the explanatory notes, to try to make them more available, less odd. For, inevitably, this anthology, which spans several centuries, traces the loss of a fundamental, music-based world-view, and its replacement by the vagaries of subjective imaginings. For J. S. Bach the trumpet was still the voice of God, the proliferating sharp signs in the 'Crucifixus' of the B minor Mass visual reminders of the points of the nails and thorns that pierced the body of the crucified Christ. Within fifty years that language was, for the most part, dead, along with the other trappings of the old world-view. Yet poets, those descendants of Orpheus, have uncanny ways of re-imagining lost fictions. Walter de la Mare, who didn't die until 1956, could still feel: 'When music sounds, all that I was I am/Ere to this haunt of brooding dust I came' ('Music').

DOUGLAS BROOKS-DAVIES

Note on the Texts

Spelling and punctuation have been modernised, except in the case of poems written over the past century or so. Where necessary, I have given sources for texts used in the Notes, and where possible the date of first publication.

What Sweeter Music

ANON

from **Sir Orfeo**

Orfeo most of any thing
Loved the glee of harping:
Siker was every good harper
Of him to have much honour.
Himself he learned for to harp   5
And laid thereon his wits sharp.
He learned so, there nothing was
A better harper in no place:
In the world was never man born
That once Orfeo sat beforn,   10
And he might of his harping hear,
He should think that he were
In one of the joys of paradise,
Such melody in his harping is . . .
And when the weather was clear and bright   15
He took his harp to him well right
And harped at his own will.
Into all the wood the sound gan shill,
That all the wild beasts that there beth
For joy abouten him they teth,   20
And all the fowls that there were
Come and sit on each a brier
To hear his harping afine,
So much melody was therein . . .

SIR THOMAS WYATT

'Blame not my Lute'

Blame not my lute, for he must sound
Of this or that as liketh me;
For lack of wit the lute is bound
To give such tunes as pleaseth me:
Though my songs be somewhat strange,   5
And speaks such words as touch thy change,
      Blame not my lute.

My lute, alas, doth not offend,
Though that perforce he must agree
To sound such tunes as I intend   10
To sing to them that heareth me:
Then though my songs be somewhat plain
And toucheth some that use to feign,
      Blame not my lute.

My lute and strings may not deny,   15
But, as I strike, they must obey:
Break not them then so wrongfully,
But wreak thyself some wiser way,
And, though the songs which I indite
Do quit thy change with rightful spite,   20
      Blame not my lute.

Spite asketh spite, and changing change,
And falsed faith must needs be known;
The fault so great, the case so strange,
Of right it must abroad be blown: 25
Then since that by thine own desert
My songs do tell how true thou art,
      Blame not my lute.

Blame but thyself that hast misdone
And well deserved to have blame: 30

Change thou thy ways so evil begun,
And then my lute shall sound that same.
But if till then my fingers play
By thy desert their wonted way,
     Blame not my lute.   35

Farewell, unknown, for though thou break
My strings in spite with great disdain,
Yet have I found out for thy sake
Strings for to string my lute again.
And if perchance this foolish rhyme   40
Do make thee blush at any time,
     Blame not my lute.

ANON

Of the Death of Phillips

Bewail with me, all ye that have professed
Of music the art by touch of cord or wind;
Lay down your lutes, and let your gitterns rest:
Phillips is dead, whose like you cannot find,
Of music much exceeding all the rest.   5
Muses, therefore of force now must you wrest
Your pleasant notes into another sound;
The string is broke, the lute is dispossessed,
The hand is cold, the body in the ground.
The louring lute lamenteth now therefore   10
Phillips her friend that can her touch no more.

EDMUND SPENSER

from **The Fairy Queen**

Eftsoons they hear a most melodious sound
   Of all that mote delight a dainty ear,
   Such as at once might not on living ground,
   Save in this paradise, be heard elsewhere:
   Right hard it was for wight which did it hear   5
   To read what manner music that mote be;
   For all that pleasing is to living ear
   Was there consorted in one harmony:
Birds, voices, instruments, winds, waters, all agree.

The joyous birds, shrouded in cheerful shade,   10
   Their notes unto the voice attempered sweet;
   The angelical, soft trembling voices made
   To the instruments divine respondence meet;
   The silver-sounding instruments did meet
   With the bass murmur of the waters' fall;   15
   The waters' fall, with difference discrete,
   Now soft, now loud, unto the winds did call;
The gentle, warbling wind low answered to all.

There, whence that music seemed heard to be,
   Was the fair witch herself now solacing   20
   With a new lover, whom, through sorcery
   And witchcraft, she from afar did thither bring:
   There she had him now laid slumbering
   In secret shade after long, wanton joys,
   Whilst round about them pleasantly did sing   25
   Many fair ladies and lascivious boys,
That ever mixed their song with light, licentious toys . . .

JOHN LYLY

Song

Pan's Syrinx was a girl indeed,
Though now she's turned into a reed.
From that dear reed Pan's pipe does come,
A pipe that strikes Apollo dumb:
Nor flute, nor lute, nor gittern can   5
So chant it as the pipe of Pan.
Cross-gartered swains, and dairy girls,
With faces smug, and round as pearls,
When Pan's shrill pipe begins to play
With dancing wear out night and day.   10
The bagpipe's drone his hum lays by
When Pan sounds up his minstrelsy –
His minstrelsy! Oh base! This quill,
Which at my mouth with wind I fill,
Puts me in mind, though her I miss,   15
That still my Syrinx' lips I kiss.

GEORGE CHAPMAN

from Ovid's Banquet of Sense

Now, Muses, come, repair your broken wings
(Plucked and profaned by rustic ignorance)
With feathers of these notes my mistress sings,
And let quick verse her drooping head advance
   From dungeons of contempt to smite the stars.   5
In Julia's tunes, led forth by furious trance,
   A thousand Muses come to bid you wars:
Dive to your spring, and hide you from the stroke,
   All poets' furies will her tunes invoke.

Never was any sense so set on fire   10
With an immortal ardour as mine ears:
Her fingers to the strings doth speech inspire,
And numbered laughter, that the descant bears
    To her sweet voice, whose species through my sense
My spirits to their highest function rears;   15
      To which impressed, with ceaseless confluence
It useth them, as proper to her power,
Marries my soul, and makes itself her dower.

Me thinks her tunes fly gilt, like Attic bees,
To my ears' hives, with honey tried to air;   20
My brain is but the comb, the wax, the lees,
My soul the drone that lives by their affair.
    Oh so it sweets, refines, and ravisheth,
And with what sport they sting in their repair!
      Rise, then, in swarms, and sting me thus to death, 25
Or turn me into swound: possess me whole,
Soul to my life, and essence to my soul.

Say, gentle Air, oh does it not thee good
Thus to be smit with her correcting voice?
Why dance ye not, ye daughters of the wood?   30
Wither for ever if not now rejoice.
    Rise, stones, and build a city with her notes,
And, notes, infuse with your most Cynthian noise.
      To all the trees, sweet flowers, and crystal flutes
That crown and made this cheerful garden quick,   35
Virtue, that every touch may make such music.

Oh that, as man is called a little world,
The world might shrink into a little man
To hear the notes about this garden hurled,
That skill dispersed in tunes so Orphean   40
    Might not be lost in smiting stocks and trees
That have no ears; but, grown as it began,
      Spread their renowns as far as Phoebus sees
Through earth's dull veins; that she like heaven might move
In ceaseless music, and be filled with love.   45

In precious incense of her holy breath
My love doth offer hecatombs of notes
To all the gods, who now despise the death
Of oxen, heifers, wethers, swine and goats.
   A sonnet in her breathing sacrificed 50
Delights them more than all beasts' bellowing throats,
   As much with heaven as with my hearing prized;
And as gilt atoms in the sun appear,
So greet these sounds the gristles of mine ear,

Whose pores do open wide to their regreet, 55
And my implanted air that air embraceth
Which they impress. I feel their nimble feet
Tread my ears' labyrinth; their sport amazeth
   They keep such measure, play themselves and dance.
And now my soul in Cupid's furnace blazeth, 60
   Wrought into fury with their dalliance:
And as the fire the parched stubble burns,
So fades my flesh, and into spirit turns.

Sweet tunes, brave issue, that from Julia come;
Shook from her brain, armed like the queen of ire; 65
For, first conceived in her mental womb,
And nourished with her soul's discursive fire,
   They grew into the power of her thought.
She gave them downy plumes from her attire,
   And them to strong imagination brought: 70
That, to her voice; wherein, most movingly,
She (blessing them with kisses) lets them fly,

Who fly rejoicing, but (like noblest minds)
In giving orders life themselves do die,
Not able to endure earth's rude unkindness, 75
Bred in my sovereign parts too tenderly;
   Oh that, as intellects themselves transit
To each intelligible quality,
   My life might pass into my love's conceit,
Thus to be formed in words, her tunes, and breath, 80
And with her kisses, sing itself to death . . .

JOSHUA SYLVESTER

Variable

Vary, re-vary; tune and tune again
  (Anon to this string, and anon to that;
Bass, treble, tenor; swift, slow, sharp and flat)
Thy one same subject in a sundry strain,
To represent, by thy so diverse ditties,   5
  The dying world's so diverse alterations:
  Yet will the world have still more variations,
And, past thy verse, thy various subject yet is.

WILLIAM SHAKESPEARE

from **The Merchant of Venice**

LORENZO. How sweet the moonlight sleeps upon this bank!
  Here will we sit, and let the sounds of music
  Creep in our ears; soft stillness and the night
  Become the touches of sweet harmony.
  Sit, Jessica; look how the floor of heaven   5
  Is thick inlaid with patens of bright gold;
  There's not the smallest orb which thou behold'st
  But in his motion like an angel sings,
  Still choiring to the young-eyed cherubins;
  Such harmony is in immortal souls;   10
  But whilst this muddy vesture of decay
  Doth grossly close it in, we cannot hear it.

[Enter musicians]

Come, ho! and wake Diana with a hymn;
With sweetest touches pierce your mistress' ear,
And draw her home with music.   15

JESSICA. I am never merry when I hear sweet music.
LORENZO. The reason is, your spirits are attentive:
    For do but note a wild and wanton herd,
    Or race of youthful and unhandled colts,
    Fetching mad bounds, bellowing and neighing loud,   20
    Which is the hot condition of their blood:
    If they but hear perchance a trumpet sound,
    Or any air of music touch their ears,
    You shall perceive them make a mutual stand,
    Their savage eyes turned to a modest gaze   25
    By the sweet power of music. Therefore the poet
    Did feign that Orpheus drew the trees, stones, and floods,
    Since nought so stockish, hard, and full of rage,
    But music for the time doth change his nature:
    The man that hath no music in himself,   30
    Nor is not moved with concord of sweet sounds,
    Is fit for treasons, stratagems, and spoils;
    The motions of his spirit are dull as night,
    And his affections dark as Erebus:
    Let no such man be trusted.   35

Sonnet 8

Music to hear, why hear'st thou music sadly?
Sweets with sweets war not, joy delights in joy:
Why lov'st thou that which thou receiv'st not gladly,
Or else receiv'st with pleasure thine annoy?
If the true concord of well-tuned sounds,   5
By unions married, do offend thine ear,
They do but sweetly chide thee, who confounds
In singleness the parts that thou should'st bear:
Mark how one string, sweet husband to another,
Strikes each in each by mutual ordering,   10
Resembling sire, and child, and happy mother
Who, all in one, one pleasing note do sing:
    Whose speechless song, being many, seeming one,
    Sings this to thee: 'Thou single wilt prove none'.

Sonnet 128

How oft when thou, my music, music play'st
Upon that blessed wood whose motion sounds
With thy sweet fingers when thou gently sway'st
The wiry concord that mine ear confounds,
Do I envy those jacks that nimble leap   5
To kiss the tender inward of thy hand,
Whilst my poor lips, which should that harvest reap,
At the wood's boldness by thee blushing stand.
To be so tickled they would change their state
And situation with those dancing chips   10.
O'er whom thy fingers walk with gentle gait,
Making dead wood more blest than living lips:
    Since saucy jacks so happy are in this,
    Give them thy fingers, me thy lips to kiss.

from **The Tempest**

Where should this music be? I' the air or the earth?
It sounds no more: and, sure, it waits upon
Some god o' the island. Sitting on a bank,
Weeping again the king my father's wrack,
This music crept by me upon the waters,   5
Allaying both their fury and my passion
With its sweet air: thence I have followed it,
Or it hath drawn me, rather. But 'tis gone . . .

THOMAS CAMPION

'When to her Lute Corinna Sings'

When to her lute Corinna sings,
Her voice revives the leaden strings,
And doth in highest notes appear
As any challenged echo clear.
But when she doth of mourning speak, 5
E'en with her sighs the strings do break.

And as her lute doth live or die,
Led by her passion, so must I.
For when of pleasure she doth sing,
My thoughts enjoy a sudden spring; 10
But if she doth of sorrow speak,
E'en from my heart the strings do break.

'Follow your Saint, follow with Accents sweet'

Follow your saint, follow with accents sweet;
Haste you, sad notes, fall at her flying feet.
There, wrapped in cloud of sorrow, pity move,
And tell the ravisher of my soul I perish for her love.
But if she scorns my never-ceasing pain, 5
Then burst with sighing in her sight, and ne'er return again.

All that I sung still to her praise did tend;
Still she was first, still she my songs did end;
Yet she my love and music both doth fly —
The music that her echo is, and beauty's sympathy. 10
Then let my notes pursue her scornful flight:
It shall suffice that they were breathed, and died for her delight.

Song

   Rose-cheeked Laura, come,
Sing thou smoothly with thy beauty's
Silent music; either other
   Sweetly gracing.

   Lovely forms do flow   5
From concent divinely framed;
Heaven is music and thy beauty's
   Birth is heavenly.

   These dull notes we sing
Discords need for help to grace them;   10
Only beauty purely loving
   Knows no discord,

   But still moves delight
Like clear springs renewed by flowing,
Ever perfect, ever in them-   15
   Selves eternal.

SIR JOHN DAVIES

from Orchestra; or, A Poem of Dancing

Thus Love taught men, and men thus learned of Love
Sweet music's sound with feet to counterfeit:
Which was long time before high-thundering Jove
Was lifted up to heaven's imperial seat;
For though by birth he were the prince of Crete,   5
   Nor Crete nor heaven should the young prince have seen
   If dancers with their timbrels had not been.

Since when all ceremonious mysteries,
All sacred orgies and religious rites,
All pomps and triumphs and solemnities,   10
All funerals, nuptials, and like public sights,
All parliaments of peace, and warlike fights,
   All learned arts, and every great affair,
   A lively shape of dancing seems to bear.

For what did he, who with his ten-tongued lute   15
Gave beasts and blocks an understanding ear;
Or rather, into bestial minds and brute
Shed and infused the beams of Reason clear?
Doubtless for men that rude and savage were
   A civil form of dancing he devised,   20
   Wherewith unto their gods they sacrificed.

So did Musaeus, so Amphion did,
And Linus with his sweet, enchanting song,
And he whose hand the Earth of monsters rid
And had men's ears fast chained to his tongue,   25
And Theseus too, his wood-born slaves among,
   Used dancing as the finest policy
   To plant religion and society.

And therefore now the Thracian Orpheus' lyre
And Hercules himself are stellified,   30
And in high heaven, amidst the starry choir,
Dancing their parts, continually do slide;
So, on the zodiac, Ganymede doth ride,
   And so is Hebe, with the Muses nine,
   For pleasing Jove with dancing, made divine. . .   35

A Hymn in Praise of Music

Praise, pleasure, profit, is that three-fold band
Which ties men's minds more fast than Gordian's knot:
Each one some draws, all three none can withstand
Of force conjoined – conquest is hardly got.
    Then music may of hearts a monarch be   5
    Wherein praise, pleasure, profit so agree.

Praiseworthy music is, for God it praiseth,
And pleasant, for brute beasts therein delight;
Great profit from it flows, for why it raiseth
The mind overwhelmed with rude passions' might: 10
    When against reason passions fond rebel,
    Music doth that confirm, and these expel.

If music did not merit endless praise,
Would heavenly spheres delight in silver round?
If joyous pleasures were not in sweet lays,   15
Would they in court and country so abound?
    And profitable needs we must that call
    Which pleasure linked with praise doth bring to all.

Heroic minds, with praises most incited,
Seek praise in music, and therein excel: 20
God man, beasts, birds, with music are delighted;
And pleasant 'tis, which pleaseth all so well:
    No greater profit is then self content,
    And this doth music bring, and care prevent.

When antique poets music's praises tell,   25
They say it beasts did please, and stones did move,
To prove more dull than stones, than beasts more fell,
Those men, which pleasing music did not love;
    They feigned it cities built, and states defended,
    To show that profit great on it depended.   30

Sweet birds (poor men's musicians) never slake
To sing sweet music's praises day and night:
The dying swans in music pleasure take
To show that it the dying can delight:
   In sickness, health, peace, war, we do it need,   35
   Which proves sweet music's profit doth exceed.

But I, by niggard praising, do dispraise
Praiseworthy music in my worthless rhyme,
Ne can the pleasing profit of sweet lays
Any save learned Muses well define: 40
   Yet all by these rude lines may clearly see,
   Praise, pleasure, profit in sweet music be.

SAMUEL ROWLEY

from **When You See Me, You Know Me**

TYE. In music may your grace ever delight,
   Though not in me: music is fit for kings,
   And not for those knows not the chime of strings.
PRINCE EDWARD. Truly, I love it; yet there are a sort,
   Seeming more pure than wise, that will upbraid at it,   5
   Calling it idle, vain, and frivolous.
TYE. Your Grace hath said; indeed, they do upbraid
   That term it so, and those that do are such
   As in themselves no happy concords hold:
   All music jars with them, but sounds of good.   10
   But would your Grace a while be patient
   In music's praise, thus will I better it:
   Music is heavenly, for in heaven is music,
   For there the seraphins do sing continually:
   And when the best was born that ever was man,   15
   A choir of angels sang for joy of it;
   What of celestial was revealed to man
   Was much of music: 'tis said the beasts did worship
   And sang before the deity supernal:

The kingly prophet sang before the ark,   20
And with his music charmed the heart of Saul;
And if the poet fail us not, my lord,
The dulcet tongue of music made the stones
To move, irrational beasts and birds to dance;
And last the trumpet's music shall awake the dead,   25
And clothe their naked bones in coats of flesh
To appear in that high house of parliament
When those that gnash their teeth at music's sound
Shall make that place where music ne'er was found.

BEN JONSON

Echo's Song

Slow, slow, fresh fount, keep time with my salt tears;
   Yet slower, yet; O faintly, gentle springs:
List to the heavy part the music bears:
   Woe weeps out her division when she sings.
        Droop, herbs and flowers;   5
        Fall, grief, in showers;
        Our beauties are not ours;
          O, I could still
(Like melting snow upon some craggy hill)
        Drop, drop, drop, drop,   10
Since nature's pride is, now, a withered daffodil.

To Alphonso Ferrabosco, on his Book

To urge, my loved Alphonso, that bold fame
Of building towns, and making wild beasts tame,
Which music had; or speak her known effects –
That she removeth cares, sadness ejects,
Declineth anger, persuades clemency,   5
Doth sweeten mirth, and heighten piety,
And is, to a body often ill-inclined
No less a sovereign cure than to the mind;
To allege that greatest men were not ashamed
Of old, even by her practice, to be famed;   10
To say, indeed, she were the soul of heaven,
That the eight spheres, no less than planets seven
Moved by her order, and the ninth, more high,
Including all, were thence called harmony –
I, yet, had uttered nothing on thy part   15
When these were but the praises of the art.
But when I have said, the proofs of all these be
Shed in thy songs: 'tis true, but short of thee.

RICHARD BARNFIELD

Sonnet

If Music and sweet Poetry agree,
As they must needs (the sister and the brother),
Then must the love be great 'twixt thee and me,
    Because thou lovest the one, and I the other.
    Dowland to thee is dear, whose heavenly touch   5
Upon the lute doth ravish human sense:
Spenser to me, whose deep conceit is such
    As, passing all conceit, needs no defence.

Thou lovest to hear the sweet melodious sound
That Phoebus' lute (the queen of music) makes: 10
And I in deep delight am chiefly drowned
   Whenas himself to singing he betakes.
     One god is god of both (as poets feign);
One knight loves both, and both in thee remain.

JOHN FLETCHER

Song

Orpheus with his lute made trees,
And the mountain tops that freeze,
   Bow themselves when he did sing.
To his music, plants and flowers
Ever sprung, as sun and showers   5
   There had made a lasting spring.

Everything that heard him play,
Even the billows of the sea,
   Hung their heads, and then lay by.
In sweet music is such art,   10
Killing care and grief of heart
   Fall asleep, or, hearing, die.

WILLIAM DRUMMOND OF HAWTHORNDEN

Sonnet 8

My lute, be as thou wast when thou didst grow
With thy green mother in some shady grove,
When immelodious winds but made thee move,
And birds on thee their ramage did bestow:
Sith that dear voice which did thy sounds approve,   5
Which used in such harmonious strains to flow,
Is reft from Earth to tune those spheres above,
What art thou but a harbinger of woe?
Thy pleasing notes be pleasing notes no more,
But orphan wailings to the fainting ear;   10
Each stop a sigh, each sound draws forth a tear.
Be therefore silent as in woods before;
    Or if that any hand to touch thee deign,
    Like widowed turtle, still her loss complain.

GEORGE WITHER

For a Musician

*Many musicians are more out of order than their instruments:
such as are so may, by singing this ode, become reprovers of
their own untuneable affections. They who are better tempered
are hereby remembered what music is most acceptable to God,
and most profitable to themselves.*

What helps it those,
        Who skill in song have found,
Well to compose
        (Of disagreeing notes)
By artful choice   5

A sweetly pleasing sound
To fit their voice
          And their melodious throats?
What helps it them
          That they this cunning know   10
If most condemn
          The way in which they go?

What will he gain
          By touching well his lute,
Who shall disdain   15
          A grave advice to hear?
What from the sounds
          Of organ, fife or lute
To him redounds
          Who doth no sin forbear?   20
A mean respect
          By tuning strings he hath
Who doth neglect
          A rectified path.

Therefore, O Lord,   25
          So tuned let me be
Unto thy Word
          And thy ten-stringed law,
That in each part
          I may thereto agree,   30
And feel my heart
          Inspired with loving awe:
He sings and plays
          The songs which best thou lovest
Who does and says   35
          The things which thou approvest.

Teach me the skill
          Of him whose harp assuaged
Those passions ill
          Which oft afflicted Saul.   40
Teach me the strain
          Which calmeth minds enraged,

And which from vain
    Affections doth recall.
So, to the choir 45
    Where angels music make,
I may aspire
    When I this life forsake.

ROBERT HERRICK

To Music

Begin to charm, and, as thou strokest mine ears
With thy enchantment, melt me into tears.
Then let thy active hand scud o'er thy lyre,
And make my spirits frantic with the fire.
That done, sink down into a silvery strain, 5
And make me smooth as balm and oil again.

To Music, to Becalm his Fever

Charm me asleep, and melt me so
    With thy delicious numbers
That, being ravished, hence I go
    Away in easy slumbers.
      Ease my sick head, 5
      And make my bed,
Thou power that canst sever
      Me from this ill,
      And quickly still,
      Thou though not kill, 10
        My fever.

Thou sweetly canst convert the same
  From a consuming fire
Into a gentle-licking flame,
    And make it thus expire.   15
      Then make me weep
      My pains asleep,
And give me such reposes
      That I, poor I,
      May think thereby   20
      I live and die
          'Mongst roses.

Fall on me like a silent dew,
  Or like those maiden showers
Which, by the peep of day, do strew   25
    A baptism o'er the flowers.
      Melt, melt my pains
      With thy soft strains
That, having ease me given,
      With full delight   30
      I leave this light,
      And take my flight
          For heaven.

Upon a Hoarse Singer

Sing me to death; for till thy voice be clear
'Twill never please the palate of mine ear.

To Mr Henry Lawes, the
Excellent Composer of his Lyrics

Touch but thy lyre, my Harry, and I hear
From thee some raptures of the rare gotire.
Then, if thy voice commingle with the string,
I hear in thee rare Lanier to sing,
Or curious Wilson. Tell me: canst thou be   5
Less than Apollo, that usurpest such three? –
Three unto whom the whole world give applause:
Yet their three praises praise but one – that's Lawes.

Upon Mr William Lawes, the Rare Musician

Should I not put on blacks when each one here
Comes with his cypress, and devotes a tear?
Should I not grieve (my Lawes) when every lute,
Viol and voice is (by thy loss) struck mute?
Thy loss, brave man! whose numbers have been hurled,   5
And no less praised, than spread throughout the world.
Some have called thee Amphion; some of us
Named thee Terpander, or sweet Orpheus –
Some this some that; but all in this agree:
Music had both her birth and death with thee.   10

THOMAS CAREW

Song. Celia Singing

You that think Love can convey
          No other way
But through the eyes into the heart
          His fatal dart,
Close up those casements and but hear   5
          This siren sing;
          And on the wing
Of her sweet voice it shall appear
That Love can enter at the ear:
          Then unveil your eyes, behold   10
          The curious mould
Where that voice dwells; and, as we know,
          When the cocks crow
          We freely may
          Gaze on the day,   15
So may you, when the music's done,
Awake and see the rising sun.

GEORGE HERBERT

Easter

Rise, heart; thy Lord is risen. Sing His praise
          Without delays
Who takes thee by the hand, that thou likewise
          With him mayest rise:
That, as His death calcined thee to dust,   5
His life may make thee gold, and much more just.

Awake, my lute, and struggle for thy part
                    With all thy art.
The cross hath taught all wood to resound His name
                    Who bore the same.   10
His stretched sinews taught all strings what key
Is best to celebrate this most high day.

Consort both heart and lute, and twist a song
                    Pleasant and long;
Or, since all music is but three parts vied   15
                    And multiplied,
O let thy blessed Spirit bear a part,
And make up our defects with His sweet art.

Church Music

Sweetest of sweets, I thank you. When displeasure
                  Did through my body wound my mind,
You took me thence, and in your house of pleasure
                  A dainty lodging me assigned.

Now I in you without a body move,
                  Rising and falling with your wings:
We both together sweetly live and love,
                  Yet say sometimes, 'God help poor kings'.

Comfort, I'll die; for if you post from me,
                  Sure I shall do so, and much more;
But if I travel in your company,
                  You know the way to heaven's door.

WILLIAM STRODE

On a Gentlewoman that Sang
and Played upon a Lute

Be silent, you still music of the spheres,
And every sense make haste to be all ears,
And give devout attention to her airs,
To which the gods do listen as to prayers
Of pious votaries, the which to hear   5
Tumult would be attentive, and would swear
To keep less noise at Nile if she would sing,
Or with a happy touch grace but the string.
Among so many auditors, so many throngs
Of gods and men that press to hear her songs,   10
Oh let me have an unespied room,
And die with such an anthem o'er my tomb.

OWEN FELTHAM

Upon a Rare Voice

When I but hear her sing, I fare
Like one that, raised, holds his ear
To some bright star in the supremest round,
Through which, besides the light that's seen,
There may be heard from heavens that within   5
The rests of anthems that the angels sound.

JOHN MILTON

from **Il Penseroso**

And when the sun begins to fling
His flaring beams, me goddess bring
To arched walks of twilight groves
And shadows brown, that Sylvan loves,
Of pine, or monumental oak,   5
Where the rude axe with heaved stroke
Was never heard the nymphs to daunt,
Or fright them from their hallowed haunt.
There in close covert by some brook,
Where no profaner eye may look,   10
Hide me from day's garish eye,
While the bee with honeyed thigh,
That at her flowery work doth sing,
And the waters murmuring
With such consort as they keep,   15
Entice the dewy-feathered Sleep;
And let some strange, mysterious dream
Wave at his wings, in airy stream
Of lively portraiture displayed,
Softly on my eyelids laid.   20
And, as I wake, sweet music breathe
Above, about, or underneath,
Sent by some spirit to mortals good,
Or the unseen genius of the wood.
But let my due feet never fail   25
To walk the studious cloister's pale,
And love the high, embowed roof,
With antique pillars' massy proof,
And storied windows richly dight,
Casting a dim, religious light.   30
There let the pealing organ blow
To the full-voiced choir below
In service high and anthems clear,
As may with sweetness through mine ear

Dissolve me into ecstasies,   35
And bring all heaven before mine eyes.

At a Solemn Music

Blest pair of sirens, pledges of heaven's joy,
Sphere-borne harmonious sisters, Voice and Verse,
Wed your divine sounds and mixed power employ,
Dead things with inbreathed sense able to pierce,
And to our high-raised fantasy present   5
That undisturbed song of pure concent
Aye sung before the sapphire-coloured throne
To Him that sits thereon
With saintly shout and solemn jubilee,
Where the bright seraphim in burning row   10
Their loud, uplifted angel trumpets blow,
And the cherubic host in thousand choirs
Touch their immortal harps of golden wires,
With those just spirits that wear victorious palms,
Hymns of devout and holy psalms   15
Sing everlastingly;
That we on earth with undiscording voice
May rightly answer that melodious noise,
As once we did, till disproportioned sin
Jarred against nature's chime, and with harsh din   20
Broke the fair music that all creatures made
To their great Lord, whose love their motion swayed
In perfect diapason whilst they stood
In first obedience, and their state of good.
Oh may we soon again renew that song   25
And keep in tune with heaven, till God ere long
To his celestial consort us unite,
To live with him, and sing in endless morn of light.

from **Paradise Lost, Book I**

Then straight [Satan] commands that at the warlike sound
Of trumpets loud and clarions be upreared
His mighty standard; that proud honour claimed
Azazel as his right, a cherub tall,
Who forthwith from the glittering staff unfurled   5
The imperial ensign, which, full high advanced,
Shone like a meteor streaming to the wind,
With gems and golden lustre rich emblazed,
Seraphic arms and trophies; all the while,
Sonorous metal blowing martial sounds: 10
At which the universal host upsent
A shout that tore hell's concave, and beyond
Frighted the reign of Chaos and old Night.
All in a moment through the gloom were seen
Ten thousand banners rise into the air   15
With orient colours waving; with them rose
A forest huge of spears; and thronging helms
Appeared, and serried shields in thick array
Of depth immeasurable. Anon they move
In perfect phalanx to the Dorian mood   20
Of flutes and soft recorders, such as raised
To heighth of noblest temper heroes old
Arming to battle, and instead of rage
Deliberate valour breathed, firm and unmoved
With dread of death to flight or foul retreat,   25
Nor wanting power to mitigate and assuage,
With solemn touches, troubled thoughts, and chase
Anguish and doubt and fear and sorrow and pain
From mortal or immortal minds.

ABRAHAM COWLEY

from **Davideis**

Tell me, O Muse – for thou or none canst tell
The mystic powers that in blest numbers dwell;
Thou their great nature knowest; nor is it fit
This noblest gem of thine own crown to omit –
Tell me from whence these heavenly charms arise: 5
Teach the dull world to admire what they despise.
   As first a various, unformed hint we find
Rise in some godlike poet's fertile mind,
Till all the parts and words their places take,
And with just marches verse and music make.   10
Such was God's poem, this world's new essay:
So wild and rude in its first draft it lay;
The ungoverned parts no correspondence knew,
And artless war from thwarting motions grew,
Till they to number and fixed rules were brought   15
By the eternal mind's poetic thought.
Water and air he for the tenor chose,
Earth made the bass, the treble flame arose;
To the active moon a quick, brisk stroke he gave,
To Saturn's string a touch more soft and grave.   20
The motions straight and round and swift and slow
And short and long were mixed and woven so,
Did in such artful figures smoothly fall,
As made this decent measured dance of all.
And this is music: sounds that charm our ears   25
Are but one dressing that rich science wears.
Though no man hear it, no man it rehearse,
Yet will there still be music in my verse.
In this great world so much of it we see;
The lesser, man, is all o'er harmony.   30
Storehouse of all proportions! Single choir!
Which first God's breath did tunefully inspire!
From hence blest music's heavenly charms arise,
From sympathy which them and man allies.

Thus they our souls, thus they our bodies win,   35
Not by their force, but party that's within.
Thus the strange cure on our spilt blood applied
Sympathy to the distant wound does guide.
Thus when two brethren strings are set alike,
To move them both, but one of them we strike: 40
Thus David's lyre did Saul's great rage control,
And tuned the harsh disorders of his soul.

ANDREW MARVELL

Music's Empire

First was the world as one great cymbal made,
Where jarring winds to infant Nature played.
All music was a solitary sound,
To hollow rocks and murmuring fountains bound.

Jubal first made the wilder notes agree;   5
And Jubal tuned music's first jubilee:
He called the echoes from their sullen cell,
And built the organ's city, where they dwell.

Each sought a consort in that lovely place,
And virgin trebles wed the manly bass;   10
From whence the progeny of numbers new
Into harmonious colonies withdrew.

Some to the lute, some to the viol went,
And others chose the cornet eloquent –
These practising wind, and those the wire,   15
To sing men's triumphs, or in heaven's choir.

Then music, the mosaic of the air,
Did of all these a solemn noise prepare,

With which she gained the empire of the ear,
Including all between the earth and sphere.   20

Victorious sounds! Yet here your homage do
Unto a gentler conqueror than you,
Who, though he flies the music of his praise,
Would with you heaven's hallelujahs raise.

HENRY VAUGHAN

The Morning Watch

O joys! Infinite sweetness! With what flowers
And shoots of glory my soul breaks and buds!
        All the long hours
        Of night and rest,
        Through the still shrouds
        Of sleep and clouds
        This dew fell on my breast.
        Oh how it bloods
And spirits all my earth! Hark – in what rings
And hymning circulations the quick world   10
        Awakes and sings!
        The rising winds,
        And falling springs,
        Birds, beasts – all things –
        Adore him in their kinds.
        Thus all is hurled
In sacred hymns and order, the great chime
And symphony of nature. Prayer is
        The world in tune,
        A spirit voice,   20
        And vocal joys
        Whose echo is heaven's bliss.
        Oh, let me climb
When I lie down! The pious soul by night

Is like a clouded star whose beams – though said
        To shed their light
        Under some cloud –
        Yet are above,
        And shine, and move
      Beyond that misty shroud.   30
        So in my bed
(That curtained grave), though sleep – like ashes – hide
My lamp and life, both shall in thee abide.

Church Service

Blest be the God of harmony and love!
        The God above!
        And holy dove!
Whose interceding spiritual groans
        Make restless moans   5
        For dust and stones,
        For dust in every part,
        But a hard, stony heart.

Oh how in this thy choir of souls I stand
        (Propped by thy hand)   10
        A heap of sand,
Which busy thoughts (like winds) would scatter quite,
        And put to flight,
        But for thy might:
        Thy hand alone doth tame
        Those blasts, and knit my frame.   15

So that both stones, and dust, and all of me
        Jointly agree
        To cry unto thee.
And in this music by thy martyrs' blood   20
        Sealed, and made good.

Present, O God,
The echo of these stones
– My sighs and groans.

THOMAS STANLEY

Celia Singing

Roses in breathing forth their scent,
Or stars their borrowed ornament;
Nymphs in the watery sphere that move,
Or angels in their orbs above;
The winged chariot of the light,   5
Or the slow, silent wheels of night;
The shade which from the swifter sun
Doth in a circular motion run;
Or souls that their eternal rest do keep,
Make far more noise than Celia's breath in sleep.   10

But if the angel which inspires
This subtle frame with active fires
Should mould this breath to words, and those
Into a harmony dispose,
The music of this heavenly sphere   15
Would steal each soul out at the ear,
And into plants and stones infuse
A life that cherubins would choose;
And with new powers invert the laws of fate,
Kill those that live, and dead things animate.   20

CLEMENT PAMAN

On Christmas Day: To my Heart

Today,
Hark! Heaven sings;
Stretch, tune, my heart!
(For hearts have strings
May bear their part)   5
And though thy lute were bruised i' the Fall,
Bruised hearts may teach an humble pastoral.

Today,
Shepherd's rejoice,
And angels do   10
No more: thy voice
Can reach that too:
Bring then at least thy pipe along
And mingle consort with the angels' song.

Today,   15
A shed that's thatched
(Yet straws can sing)
Holds God; God matched
With beasts; beasts bring
Their song their way: for shame, then, raise   20
Thy notes! Lambs bleat, and oxen bellow praise.

Today,
God honoured man
Not angels: yet
They sing; and can   25
Raised man forget?
Praise is our debt today; now shall
Angels (man's not so poor) discharge it all?

> Today,
> Then, screw thee high,   30
> My heart, up to
> The angels' key;
> Sing 'Glory,' do:
> What if thy strings all crack and fly?
> On such a ground, music 'twill be to die.   35

JOHN DRYDEN

A Song for St Cecilia's Day, 1687

From harmony, from heavenly harmony
   This universal frame began.
   When Nature underneath a heap
     Of jarring atoms lay,
   And could not heave her head,   5
The tuneful voice was heard from high,
     'Arise, ye more than dead.'
Then cold and hot, and moist and dry,
In order to their stations leap,
     And MUSIC's power obey.   10
From harmony to heavenly harmony
   This universal frame began:
   From harmony to harmony,
Through all the compass of the notes it ran,
The diapason closing full in man.   15

What passion cannot MUSIC raise and quell!
   When Jubal struck the corded shell,
   His listening brethren stood around
   And, wondering, on their faces fell
   To worship that celestial sound.   20
Less than a god they thought there could not dwell
   Within the hollow of that shell
   That spoke so sweetly and so well.
What passion cannot MUSIC raise and quell!

The TRUMPET's loud clangour   25
    Excites us to arms
    With shrill notes of anger
    And mortal alarms.
    The double, double beat
    Of the thundering DRUM   30
    Cries 'Hark, the foes come;
Charge, charge, 'tis too late to retreat!'

    The soft complaining FLUTE
    In dying notes discovers
    The woes of hopeless lovers,   35
Whose dirge is whispered by the warbling LUTE.

    Sharp VIOLINS proclaim
Their jealous pangs and desperation
Fury, frantic indignation,
Depth of pains, and height of passion   40

    For the fair, disdainful dame.
    But oh! what art can teach,
    What human voice can reach,
The sacred ORGAN's praise?
Notes inspiring holy love,   45
Notes that wing their heavenly ways
    To mend the choirs above.

Orpheus could lead the savage race;
And trees unrooted left their place,
    Sequacious of the lyre;   50
But bright CECILIA raised the wonder higher:
When to her ORGAN vocal breath was given
An angel heard, and straight appeared,
    Mistaking Earth for heaven.

    Grand CHORUS

    As from the power of sacred lays   55
     The spheres began to move.
    And sung the great Creator's praise

> *To all the bless'd above,*
> *So when the last and dreadful hour*
> *This crumbling pageant shall devour,*　　　　60
> *The* TRUMPET *shall be heard on high,*
> *The dead shall live, the living die,*
> *And* MUSIC *shall untune the sky.*

An Ode, on the Death of Mr Henry Purcell,
Late Servant to His Majesty, and Organist of the Chapel Royal, and of St Peter's, Westminster

> Mark how the lark and linnet sing:
> 　With rival notes
> They strain their warbling throats
> 　To welcome in the spring.
> 　But in the close of night,　　　　5
> When Philomel begins her heavenly lay,
> 　They cease their mutual spite,
> 　Drink in her music with delight,
> And, listening and silent, and silent and
> 　　listening,
> 　And listening and silent obey.　　　　10
>
> So ceased the rival crew when Purcell came:
> They sung no more, or only sung his fame.
> Struck dumb, they all admired the godlike man –
> 　The godlike man
> 　Alas too soon retired　　　　15
> 　As he too late began.
> We beg not hell our Orpheus to restore:
> 　Had he been there,
> 　Their sovereign fear
> 　Had sent him back before.　　　　20
> The power of harmony too well they know:
> He long ere this had tuned their jarring sphere
> 　And left no hell below.

The heavenly choir, who heard his notes from high,
Let down the scale of music from the sky: 25
    They handed him along,
And all the way he taught, and all the way they sung.
Ye brethren of the lyre and tuneful voice,
Lament his lot: but at your own rejoice.
Now live secure and linger out your days: 30
The gods are pleased alone with Purcell's lays,
    Nor know to mend their choice.

SAMUEL PORDAGE

To Lucia Playing her Lute

When last I heard your nimble fingers play
Upon your lute, nothing so sweet as they
Seemed: all my soul fled ravished to my ear,
That sweetly animating sound to hear.
My ravished heart with play kept equal time,   5
Fell down with you, with you did ela climb;
Grew sad or lighter, as the tunes you played;
And with your lute a perfect measure made:
If all, so much as I, your music love,
The whole world would at your devotion move,   10
And, at your speaking lute's surpassing charms,
Embrace a lasting peace, and fling by arms.

JOHN WILMOT, EARL OF ROCHESTER

Spoken Extempore to a Country Clerk, after Hearing Him Sing Psalms

Sternhold and Hopkins had great qualms
When they translated David's psalms
   To make the heart full glad.
But had it been poor David's fate
To hear thee sing, and them translate,   5
   By God, 'twould have made him mad.

AMBROSE PHILIPS

To Signora Cuzzoni

Little siren of the stage,
Charmer of an idle age,
Empty warbler, breathing lyre,
Wanton gale of fond desire,
Bane of every manly art,   5
Sweet enfeebler of the heart:
Oh, too pleasing is thy strain!
Hence, to southern climes again:
Tuneful mischief, vocal spell,
To this island bid farewell.   10
Leave us as we ought to be –
Leave the Britons rough and free.

ALEXANDER POPE

from **The Dunciad**

When lo! a harlot form soft sliding by,
With mincing step, small voice, and languid eye:
Foreign her air, her robe's discordant pride
In patchwork fluttering, and her head aside;
By singing peers upheld on either hand,   5
She tripped and laughed, too pretty much to stand;
Cast on the prostrate nine a scornful look,
Then thus in quaint recitativo spoke:
   'Oh cara, cara! silence all that train:
Joy to great Chaos! let division reign!   10
Chromatic tortures soon shall drive them hence,
Break all their nerves, and fritter all their sense:
One trill shall harmonise joy, grief, and rage,
Wake the dull Church, and lull the ranting stage.
To the same notes thy sons shall hum or snore,   15
And all thy yawning daughters cry "encore."
Another Phoebus – thy own Phoebus – reigns,
Joys in my jigs and dances in my chains.
But soon, ah, soon, rebellion will commence,
If music meanly borrows aid from sense: 20
Strong in new arms, lo, giant Handel stands,
Like bold Briareus, with a hundred hands:
To stir, to rouse, to shake the soul he comes,
And Jove's own thunders follow Mars's drums . . .'

JOHN BYROM

Epigram on Handel and Bononcini

Some say, compared to Bononcini,
That Mynheer Handel's but a ninny;
Others aver that he to Handel
Is scarcely fit to hold a candle.
Strange all this difference should be   5
'Twixt Tweedle-dum and Tweedle-dee!

HENRIETTA KNIGHT, LADY LUXBOROUGH

The Bullfinch in Town

Hark to the blackbird's pleasing note,
    Sweet usher of the vocal throng!
Nature directs her warbling note,
    And all that hear admire the song.

Yon bullfinch, with unvaried tone   5
    Of cadence harsh and accent shrill,
Has brighter plumage to atone
    For want of harmony and skill.

Yet, discontent with nature's boon,
    Like man to mimic art he flies,   10
On opera pinions hoping soon
    Unrivalled he shall mount the skies.

And while, to please some courtly fair,
    He one dull tune with labour learns,
A well-gilt cage remote from air,   15
    And faded plumes, is all he earns.

Go, hapless captive! still repeat
   The sounds which nature never taught;
Go, listening fair, and call them sweet,
   Because you know them dearly bought.   20

Unenvied both! go hear and sing
   Your studied music o'er and o'er,
Whilst I attend the inviting spring
   In fields where birds unfettered soar.

JAMES MILLER

from **Harlequin-Horace**

In days of old, when Englishmen were – men,
Their music, like themselves, was grave and plain:
The manly trumpet and the simple reed
Alike with citizen and swain agreed,
Whose songs, in lofty sense but humble verse,   5
Their loves and wars alternately rehearse;
Sung by themselves, their homely cheer to crown,
In tunes from sire to son delivered down.
   But now, since Britons are become polite,
Since few can read, and fewer still can write;   10
Since travelling has so much improved our beaux,
That each brings home a foreign tongue – or nose;
And ladies paint with that amazing grace
That their best vizard is their natural face;
Since South Sea schemes have so enriched the land   15
That footmen 'gainst their lord for borough stand;
Since masquerades and operas made their entry,
And Heidegger reigned guardian of our gentry,
A hundred various instruments combine,
And foreign singers in the concert join: 20
The Gallic horn, whose winding tube in vain
Pretends to emulate the trumpet's strain;

The shrill-toned fiddle, and the warbling flute,
The grave bassoon, deep bass, and tinkling lute,
The jingling spinet and the full-mouthed drum,   25
A Roman capon and Venetian strum,
All league melodious nonsense to dispense,
And give us sound and show instead of sense;
In unknown tongues mysterious Dullness chant,
Make love in tune, or through the gamut rant.   30

SAMUEL JOHNSON

An Epitaph upon the Celebrated Claudy Philips, Musician, who died very Poor

Philips, whose touch harmonious could remove
The pangs of guilty power and hapless love,
Rest here, distressed by poverty no more:
Here find that calm thou gavest so oft before.
Sleep undisturbed within this peaceful shrine,   5
Till angels wake thee with a note like thine.

CHRISTOPHER SMART

from Jubilate Agno

For the spiritual music is as follows:
For there is the thunder-stop, which is the voice of God direct.
For the rest of the stops are by their rhymes.
For the trumpet rhymes are bound, soar, more and the like.

For the shawm rhymes are lawn, fawn, moon, boom and the
    like. 5
For the harp rhymes are sing, ring, string and the like.
For the cymbal rhymes are bell, well, toll, soul and the like.
For the flute rhymes are tooth, youth, suit, mute and the like.
For the dulcimer rhymes are grace, place, beat, heat and the
    like.
For the clarinet rhymes are clean, seen and the like. 10
For the bassoon rhymes are pass, class, and the like. God be
    gracious to Baumgarden.
For the dulcimer are rather van, fan and the like and grace,
    place etc. are of the bassoon.
For beat, heat, weep, peep, etc. are of the pipe.
For every word has its marrow in the English tongue for order
    and for delight.
For the dissyllables such as able, table, etc. are the fiddle
    rhymes. 15
For all dissyllables and some trisyllables are fiddle rhymes.

ANNA SEWARD

Epitaph for John Saville

Once in the heart cold in yon narrow cell
Did each mild grace, each ardent virtue dwell;
Kind, and kind tears for others' want and woe.
For others' joy the gratulating glow,
And skill to mark and eloquence to claim 5
For genius in each art the palm of fame.
Ye choral walls, ye lost the matchless song
When the last silence stiffened on that tongue.
Ah, who may now your pealing anthems raise
In soul-poured tones of fervent prayer and praise? 10
Saville, thy lips twice on their final day
Here breathed, in health and hope, the sacred lay;
Short pangs, ere night, their fatal signal gave,
Quenched the bright sun for thee – and oped the grave.

Now from that graceful form and beaming face   15
Insatiate worms the lingering likeness chase.
But thy pure spirit fled from pains and fears
To sinless, changeless, everlasting spheres.
Sleep then, pale, mortal frame, in yon low shrine
Till angels wake thee with a note like thine.   20

WILLIAM BLAKE

Song

There's Doctor Clash,
And Signior Falalasole:
Oh, they sweep in the cash
Into their purse hole,
Fa me la sol, La me fa sol.   5

Great A, little A,
Bouncing B,
Play away, play away –
You're out of the key,
Fa me la sol, La me fa sol.   10

Musicians should have
A pair of very good ears,
And long fingers and thumbs,
And not like clumsy bears,
Fa me la sol, La me fa sol.   15

Gentlemen, gentlemen,
Rap, rap, rap,
Fiddle, fiddle, fiddle,
Clap, clap, clap,
Fa me la sol, La me fa sol.   20

WILLIAM LISLE BOWLES

At Ostend, July 22, 1787

How sweet the tuneful bells' responsive peal:
   As when, at opening morn, the fragrant breeze
   Breathes on the trembling sense of wan disease,
So piercing to my heart their force I feel!
   And hark! with lessening cadence now they fall,   5
And now, along the white and level tide,
They fling their melancholy music wide,
   Bidding me many a tender thought recall
Of summer days, and those delightful years
   When by my native streams, in life's fair prime,   10
   The mournful magic of their mingling chime
First waked my wondering childhood into tears –
   But seeming now, when all those days are o'er,
   The sounds of joy, once heard, and heard no more.

WILLIAM WORDSWORTH

from **On the Power of Sound**

The gift to King Amphion
That walled a city with its melody
Was for belief no dream: thy skill, Arion,
Could humanise the creatures of the sea,
Where men were monsters. A last grace he craves –   5
Leave for one chant. The dulcet sound
Steals from the deck o'er willing waves,
And listening dolphins gather round.
Self-cast, as with a desperate course,
'Mid that strange audience, he bestrides   10
A proud one docile as a managed horse;

And singing, while the accordant hand
Sweeps his harp, the master rides.
So shall he touch at length a friendly strand,
And he, with his preserver, shine star-bright   15
In memory, through silent night.

The pipe of Pan, to shepherds
Couched in the shadow of Maenalian pines,
Was passing sweet; the eyeballs of the leopards,
That in high triumph drew the lord of vines,   20
How did they sparkle to the cymbals' clang,
While fauns and satyrs beat the ground
In cadence, and Silenus swang
This way and that, with wild flowers crowned.
To life, to *life* give back thine ear: 25
Ye who are longing to be rid
Of fable, though to truth subservient, hear
The little sprinkling of cold earth that fell
Echoed from the coffin lid;
The convict's summons in the steeple's knell;   30
The vain distress gun, from a leeward shore,
Repeated – heard, and heard no more!

From terror, joy, or pity,
Vast is the compass and the swell of notes:
From the babe's first cry to voice of regal city,   35
Rolling a solemn sea-like bass, that floats
Far as the woodlands – with the trill to blend
Of that shy songstress, whose love tale
Might tempt an angel to descend,
While hovering o'er the moonlight vale.   40
Ye wandering utterances, has earth no scheme,
No scale of moral music, to unite
Powers that survive but in the faintest dream
Of memory? Oh that ye might stoop to bear
Chains, such precious chains of sight   45
As laboured minstrelsies through ages wear!
Oh for a balance fit the truth to tell
Of the unsubstantial, pondered well!

By one pervading spirit
Of tones and numbers all things are controlled,   50
As sages taught, where faith was found to merit
Initiation in that mystery old.
The heavens, whose aspect makes our minds as still
As they themselves appear to be,
Innumerable voices fill   55
With everlasting harmony;
The towering headlands, crowned with mist,
Their feet among the billows, know
That Ocean is a mighty harmonist;
Thy pinions, universal air,   60
Ever waving to and fro,
Are delegates of harmony, and bear
Strains that support the seasons in their round;
Stern Winter loves a dirge-like sound.

Break forth into thanksgiving,   65
Ye banded instruments of wind and chords;
Unite, to magnify the Ever-living,
Your inarticulate notes with the voice of words!
Nor hushed be service from the lowing mead,
Nor mute the forest hum of noon;   70
Thou too be heard, lone eagle! Freed
From snowy peak and cloud, attune
Thy hungry barkings to the hymn
Of joy that from her utmost walls
The six-days' work by flaming seraphim   75
Transmits to heaven! As deep to deep
Shouting through one valley calls,
All worlds, all natures, mood and measure keep
For praise and ceaseless gratulation, poured
Into the ear of God, their Lord . . .   80

The Solitary Reaper

Behold her, single in the field,
Yon solitary highland lass!
Reaping and singing by herself;
Stop here, or gently pass!
Alone she cuts and binds the grain,   5
And sings a melancholy strain;
O listen! for the vale profound
Is overflowing with the sound.

No nightingale did ever chant
More welcome notes to weary bands   10
Of travellers in some shady haunt,
Among Arabian sands;
A voice so thrilling ne'er was heard
In spring-time from the cuckoo bird,
Breaking the silence of the seas   15
Among the farthest Hebrides.

Will no one tell me what she sings? –
Perhaps the plaintive numbers flow
For old, unhappy, far-off things,
And battles long ago: 20
Or is it some more humble lay,
Familiar matter of today?
Some natural sorrow, loss, or pain,
That has been, and may be again?

Whate'er the theme, the maiden sang   25
As if her song could have no ending;
I saw her singing at her work,
And o'er the sickle bending; –
I listened, motionless and still;
And, as I mounted up the hill,   30
The music in my heart I bore,
Long after it was heard no more.

Sonnet: Inside of King's College Chapel, Cambridge

Tax not the royal saint with vain expense;
With ill-matched aims the architect who planned –
Albeit labouring for a scanty band
Of white-robed scholars only – this immense
And glorious work of fine intelligence!   5
Give all thou canst: high heaven rejects the lore
Of nicely-calculated less or more.
So deemed the man who fashioned for the sense
These lofty pillars, spread that branching roof
Self-poised, and scooped into ten thousand cells,   10
Where light and shade repose, where music dwells
Lingering – and wandering on as loath to die:
Like thoughts whose very sweetness yieldeth proof
That they were born for immortality.

The Same

What awful perspective! While from our sight
With gradual stealth the lateral windows hide
The portraitures, their stone-work glimmers, dyed
In the soft chequerings of a sleepy light.
Martyr, or king, or sainted eremite,   5
Whoe'er ye be, that thus, yourselves unseen,
Imbue your prison bars with solemn sheen,
Shine on, until ye fade with coming night!
But from the arms of silence – list! oh list!
The music bursteth into second life;   10
The notes luxuriate, every stone is kissed
By sound, or ghost of sound, in mazy strife;
Heart-thrilling strains, that cast, before the eye
Of the devout, a veil of ecstasy!

SAMUEL TAYLOR COLERIDGE

Ode on the Ottery and Tiverton Church Music

Hence, soul-dissolving Harmony,
   That'd lead'st th' oblivious soul astray –
Though thou sphere-descended be –
   Hence away! –
Thou mightier goddess, thou demand'st my lay,   5
   Born when the Earth was seized with colic;
Or, as more sapient sages say,
   What time the Legion diabolic
      Compelled their beings to enshrine
      In bodies vile of herded swine,   10
      Precipitate adown the steep
      With hideous rout were plunging in the deep,
And hog and devil mingling grunt and yell
   Seized on the ear with horrible obtrusion; –
Then, if aright old legendaries tell,   15
   Wert thou begot by Discord on Confusion!

What though no name's sonorous power
Was given thee at thy natal hour –
Yet oft I feel thy sacred might;
While concords wing their distant flight.   20
   Such power inspires thy holy son,
     Sable clerk of Tiverton!
And oft where Otter sports his stream,
I hear thy banded offspring scream.
Thou, goddess, thou inspir'st each throat: 25
'Tis thou who pour'st the screech-owl note,
Transported hear'st thy children all
Scrape and blow and squeak and squall,
And, while old Otter's steeple rings,
Clappest hoarse thy raven wings.   30

The Aeolian Harp

Composed 20 August 1795 at Clevedon, Somersetshire

My pensive Sara! thy soft cheek reclined
Thus on mine arm, most soothing sweet it is
To sit beside our cot, our cot o'ergrown
With white-flowered jasmine and the broad-leaved myrtle
(Meet emblems they of innocence and love!)   5
And watch the clouds, that late were rich with light,
Slow saddening round, and mark the star of eve
Serenely brilliant (such should wisdom be)
Shine opposite! How exquisite the scents
Snatched from yon bean-field! And the world so hushed!   10
The stilly murmur of the distant sea
Tells us of silence. And that simplest lute,
Placed lengthways in the clasping casement, hark!
How, by the desultory breeze caressed,
Like some coy maid half-yielding to her lover,   15
It pours such sweet upbraidings as must needs
Tempt to repeat the wrong! And now, its strings
Boldlier swept, the long sequacious notes
Over delicious surges sink and rise:
Such a soft, floating witchery of sound   20
As twilight elfins make, when they at eve
Voyage on gentle gales from fairy land,
Where melodies round honey-dropping flowers,
Footless and wild, like birds of paradise,
Nor pause, nor perch, hovering on untamed wing.   25
Oh, the one life within us and abroad,
Which meets all motion and becomes its soul,
A light in sound, a sound-like power in light,
Rhythm in all thought, and joyance everywhere –
Methinks it should have been impossible   30
Not to love all things in a world so filled;
Where the breeze warbles, and the mute still air
Is Music slumbering on her instrument.
And thus, my love, as on the midway slope

Of yonder hill I stretch my limbs at noon,   35
Whilst through my half-closed eyelids I behold
The sunbeams dance, like diamonds, on the main,
And tranquil muse upon tranquillity;
Full many a thought uncalled and undetained,
And many idle, flitting fantasies,   40
Traverse my indolent and passive brain
As wild and various as the random gales
That swell or flutter on this subject lute!
And what if all of animated nature
Be but organic harps diversely framed,   45
That tremble into thought as o'er them sweeps,
Plastic and vast, one intellectual breeze,
At once the soul of each and God of all?
But thy more serious eye a mild reproof
Darts, O beloved woman! nor such thoughts   50
Dim and unhallowed dost thou not reject,
And biddest me walk humbly with my God.

Meek daughter in the family of Christ,
Well hast thou said, and holily dispraised
These shapings of the unregenerate mind,   55
Bubbles that glitter as they rise and break
On vain philosophy's aye-babbling spring.
For never guiltless may I speak of Him,
The INCOMPREHENSIBLE, save when with awe
I praise Him, and with faith that inly *feels*;   60
Who with his saving mercies healed me,
A sinful and most miserable man,
Wildered and dark, and gave me to possess
PEACE, and this COT, and THEE, heart-honoured maid!

On a Volunteer Singer

Swans sing before they die – 'twere no bad thing
Should certain persons die before they sing.

Lines Composed in a Concert Room

Nor cold, nor stern, my soul! yet I detest
  These scented rooms where, to a gaudy throng,
Heaves the proud harlot her distended breast
  In intricacies of laborious song.

These feel not music's genuine power, nor deign   5
  To melt at Nature's passion-warbled plaint;
But when the long-breathed singer's uptrilled strain
  Bursts in a squall – they gape for wonderment.

Hark! the deep buzz of vanity and hate!
Scornful yet envious, with self-torturing sneer   10
My lady eyes some maid of humbler state,
  While the pert captain, or the primmer priest,
  Prattles accordant scandal in her ear.

Oh give me, from this heartless scene released,
  To hear our old musician, blind and grey   15
(Whom stretching from my nurse's arms I kissed),
  His Scottish tunes and warlike marches play
By moonshine on the balmy summer night,
  The while I dance amid the tedded hay
With merry maids whose ringlets toss in light.   20

Or lies the purple evening on the bay
Of the calm, glossy lake: oh let me hide
  Unheard, unseen, behind the alder trees,
For round their roots the fisher's boat is tied,
  On whose trim seat doth Edmund stretch at ease,   25
And while the lazy boat sways to and fro,
  Breathes in his flute sad airs, so wild and slow,
That his own cheek is wet with quiet tears.

But oh. dear Anne, when midnight wind careers,
And the gust pelting on the outhouse shed   30
  Makes the cock shrilly in the rainstorm crow.

To hear thee sing some ballad full of woe –
Ballad of shipwrecked sailor floating dead,
    Whom his own true-love buried in the sands!
Thee, gentle woman, for thy voice remeasures   35
Whatever tones and melancholy pleasures
    The things of nature utter: birds or trees,
Or moan of ocean gale in weedy caves,
Or where the stiff grass mid the heath plant waves,
    Murmur and music thin of sudden breeze.   40

GEORGE GORDON, LORD BYRON

'The Harp the Monarch Minstrel Swept'

The harp the monarch minstrel swept,
    The king of men, the loved of heaven,
Which Music hallowed while she wept
    O'er tones her heart of hearts had given –
    Redoubled be her tears, its chords are riven!   5
It softened men of iron mould,
    It gave them virtues not their own;
No ear so dull, no soul so cold,
    That felt not, fired not, to the tone,
    Till David's lyre grew mightier than his throne!   10

It told the triumphs of our king,
    It wafted glory to our God;
It made our gladdened valleys ring,
    The cedars bow, the mountains nod;
    Its sound aspired to heaven and there abode!   15
Since then, though heard on earth no more,
    Devotion and her daughter, Love,
Still bid the bursting spirit soar
    To sounds that seem as from above,
    In dreams that day's broad light cannot remove.   20

PERCY BYSSHE SHELLEY

To —

Music, when soft voices die,
Vibrates in the memory –
Odours, when sweet violets sicken,
Live within the sense they quicken.

Rose leaves, when the rose is dead,   5
Are heaped for the beloved's bed;
And so thy thoughts, when thou art gone,
Love itself shall slumber on.

Lines: 'When the Lamp is Shattered'

When the lamp is shattered
The light in the dust lies dead –
When the cloud is scattered
The rainbow's glory is shed.
When the lute is broken,   5
Sweet tones are remembered not:
When the lips have spoken,
Loved accents are soon forgot.

As music and splendour
Survive not the lamp and the lute.   10
The heart's echoes render
No song when the spirit is mute: –
No song but sad dirges.
Like the wind through a ruined cell.
Or the mournful surges   15
That ring the dead seaman's knell.

When hearts have once mingled
Love first leaves the well-built nest;
　　The weak one is singled
To endure what it once possessed.   20
　　O Love, who bewailest
The frailty of all things here,
　　Why choose you the frailest
For your cradle, your home, and your bier?

　　Its passions will rock thee   25
As the storms rock the ravens on high;
　　Bright reason will mock thee,
Like the sun from a wintry sky.
　　From thy nest every rafter
Will rot, and thine eagle home   30
　　Leave thee naked to laughter,
When leaves fall and cold winds come.

With a Guitar, to Jane

Ariel to Miranda: – Take
This slave of Music for the sake
Of him who is the slave of thee,
And teach it all the harmony
In which thou canst, and only thou,   5
Make the delighted spirit glow,
Till joy denies itself again,
And, too intense, is turned to pain;
For by permission and command
Of thine own Prince Ferdinand,   10
Poor Ariel sends this silent token
Of more than ever can be spoken;
Your guardian spirit Ariel, who,
From life to life, must still pursue
Your happiness; for thus alone   15
Can Ariel ever find his own.

From Prospero's enchanted cell,
As the mighty verses tell,
To the throne of Naples, he
Lit you o'er the trackless sea,   20
Flitting on, your prow before,
Like a living meteor.
When you die, the silent Moon,
In her interlunar swoon,
Is not sadder in her cell   25
Than deserted Ariel.
When you live again on earth,
Like an unseen star of birth,
Ariel guides you o'er the sea
Of life from your nativity.   30
Many changes have been run
Since Ferdinand and you begun
Your course of love, and Ariel still
Has tracked your steps, and served your will.
Now, in humbler, happier lot,   35
This is all remembered not;
And now, alas! the poor sprite is
Imprisoned for some fault of his,
In a body like a grave;
From you he only dares to crave,   40
For his service and his sorrow,
A smile today, a song tomorrow.

The artist who this idol wrought,
To echo all harmonious thought,
Felled a tree, while on the steep   45
The woods were in their winter sleep,
Rocked in that repose divine
On the windswept Apennine,
And dreaming – some of autumn past,
And some of spring approaching fast,   50
And some of April buds and showers,
And some of songs in July bowers,
And all of love; and so this tree –
Oh that such our death may be! –
Died in sleep, and felt no pain,   55

To live in happier form again:
From which, beneath heaven's fairest star,
The artist wrought this loved guitar,
And taught it justly to reply
To all who question skilfully,   60
In language gentle as thine own;
Whispering in enamoured tone
Sweet oracles of woods and dells,
And summer winds in sylvan cells.
For it had learned all harmonies   65
Of the plains and of the skies,
Of the forests and the mountains,
And the many-voiced fountains;
The clearest echoes of the hills,
The softest notes of falling rills,   70
The melodies of birds and bees,
The murmuring of summer seas,
And pattering rain, and breathing dew,
And airs of evening; and it knew
That seldom-heard mysterious sound,   75
Which, driven on its diurnal round,
As it floats through boundless day,
Our world enkindles on its way.
All this it knows, but will not tell
To those who cannot question well   80
The spirit that inhabits it;
It talks according to the wit
Of its companions; and no more
Is heard than has been felt before,
By those who tempt it to betray   85
These secrets of an elder day:
But, sweetly as its answers will
Flatter hands of perfect skill,
It keeps its highest, holiest tone
For our beloved Jane alone   90

THOMAS LOVELL BEDDOES

Hymn

And many voices marshalled in one hymn
Wound through the night, whose still, translucent moments
Lay on each side their breath; and the hymn passed
Its long, harmonious populace of words
Between the silvery silences, as when
The slaves of Egypt, like a wind between
The head and trunk of a dismembered king
On a strewn plank, with blood and footsteps sealed,
Valleyed the unaccustomed sea.

ALFRED, LORD TENNYSON

Song

It is the solemn even-time,
   And the holy organ's pealing:
And the vesper-chime, oh! the vesper-chime!
   O'er the clear blue wave is stealing.

It is the solemn mingled swell   5
   Of the monks in chorus singing:
And the vesper-bell, oh! the vesper-bell!
   To the gale is its soft note flinging.

'Tis the sound of the voices sweeping along,   10
   Like the wind through a grove of larches:
And the vesper-song, oh! the vesper-song.
   Echoes sad through the cloistered arches.

The Dying Swan

The plain was grassy, wild and bare
Wide, wild, and open to the air,
Which had built up everywhere
   An under-roof of doleful grey.
With an inner voice the river ran,   5
Adown it floated a dying swan,
   And loudly did lament.
It was the middle of the day.
Ever the weary wind went on,
   And took the reed-tops as it went.   10

Some blue peaks in the distance rose,
And white against the cold-white sky
Shone out their crowning snows.
   One willow over the river wept,
And shook the wave as the wind did sigh;   15
Above in the wind was the swallow,
      Chasing itself at its own wild will,
        And far through the marish green and still
      The tangled water-courses slept,
Shot over with purple, and green, and yellow.   20

The wild swan's death hymn took the soul
Of that waste place with joy
Hidden in sorrow: at first to the ear
The warble was low, and full and clear;
And floating about the under-sky,   25
Prevailing in weakness, the coronach stole
Sometimes afar, and sometimes anear;
But anon her awful jubilant voice,
With a music strange and manifold,
Flowed forth on a carol free and bold;   30
As when a mighty people rejoice
With shawms, and with cymbals, and harps of gold,
And the tumult of their acclaim is rolled
Through the open spaces of the city afar,

To the shepherd who watcheth the evening star.   35
And the creeping mosses and clambering weeds,
And the willow-branches hoar and dank,
And the wavy swell of the soughing reeds,
And the wave-worn horns of the echoing bank,
And the silvery marish-flowers that throng   40
The desolate creeks and the pools among,
Were flooded over with eddying song.

'The Splendour Falls on Castle Walls'

The splendour falls on castle walls
    And snowy summits old in story:
The long light shakes across the lakes,
    And the wild cataract leaps in glory.
Blow, bugle, blow, set the wild echoes flying,   5
Blow, bugle; answer, echoes, dying, dying, dying.

O hark, O hear! how thin and clear,
    And thinner, clearer, farther going!
O sweet and far from cliff and scar
    The horns of Elfland sweetly blowing!   10
Blow, let us hear the purple glens replying:
Blow, bugle; answer, echoes, dying, dying, dying.

O love, they die in yon rich sky,
    They faint on hill or field or river:
Our echoes roll from soul to soul,   15
    And grow for ever and for ever.
Blow, bugle, blow, set the wild echoes flying,
And answer, echoes, answer, dying, dying, dying.

Orlando Gibbons

Thy voice, great Master, echoes through the soul,
While churches last, quires chant, and organs roll!

WILLIAM BELL SCOTT

Music

Listless the silent ladies sit
About the room so gaily lit;
Madame Ions likes the cups or ray,
But thinks it scarce enough to say:
Mistress Cox is gone astray   5
To the night-light in her own nursery,
Wonders if little Maude was led
Without long coaxing into bed:
Miss Jemima Applewhite,
On a low stool by the fire,   10
Concentrates her confused desire, –
Perhaps will do so all the night,
On an unused rhyme for 'scan',
And can but find the stiff word *man*:
Miss Temple pets the little hound,   15
That has a tendency to whine,
To-night its cushions can't be found;
And wonders when they'll leave the wine
Few take, but which men still combine
To linger over when they dine.   20
Indeed a frightful interval!
Madame Ions wants her game,
Or she must have her usual wink:
But now satiric Bertha Stahl
Jumps upon the music-stool,   25

And breaks into a sportive flame;
But what of all things do you think
She plays, that laughter-loving fool?
The funeral march, Dead March of Saul!

O, Lord of Hosts! their mailèd tread   30
Bearing along the mailèd dead,
Makes me bow my stubborn head.
Never underneath the sun
With this heart-fathoming march be done;
Still, Lord of Hosts! to Thee we cry,   35
When our great ones, loved ones, die,
Still some grand lament we crave,
When we descend into the grave.

I turn, afraid that I may weep, –
Jemima's pestered wits still ran   40
After the unused rhyme for 'scan',
Dear old Ions was still asleep.

ROBERT BROWNING

Abt Vogler
(After he has been Extemporising Upon the Musical Instrument of his Invention)

Would that the structure brave, the manifold music I build,
    Bidding my organ obey, calling the keys to their work,
Claiming each slave of the sound, at a touch, as when Solomon
        willed
    Armies of angels that soar, legions of demons that lurk,
Man, brute, reptile, fly, – alien of end and of aim,   5
    Adverse, each from the other heaven-high, hell-deep
        removed, –
Should rush into sight at once as he named the ineffable Name,

And pile him a palace straight, to pleasure the princess he
    loved!

Would it might tarry like his, the beautiful building of mine,
    This which my keys in a crowd pressed and importuned to
    raise!   10
Ah, one and all, how they helped, would dispart now and now
    combine,
    Zealous to hasten the work, heighten their master his praise!
And one would bury his brow with a blind plunge down to hell,
    Burrow awhile and build, broad on the roots of things,
Then up again swim into sight, having based me my palace
    well,   15
    Founded it, fearless of flame, flat on the nether springs.

And another would mount and march, like the excellent minion
    he was,
    Aye, another and yet another, one crowd but with many a
    crest,
Raising my rampired walls of gold as transparent as glass,
    Eager to do and die, yield each his place to the rest: 20
For higher still and higher (as a runner tips with fire,
    When a great illumination surprises a festal night –
Outlining round and round Rome's dome from space to spire)
    Up, the pinnacled glory reached, and the pride of my soul was
    in sight.

In sight? Not half! For it seemed, it was certain, to match man's
    birth,   25
    Nature in turn conceived, obeying an impulse as I;
And the emulous heaven yearned down, made effort to reach the
    earth,
    As the earth had done her best, in my passion, to scale the sky:
Novel splendours burst forth, grew familiar and dwelt with mine,
    Not a point nor peak but found and fixed its wandering star: 30
Meteor-pointed moons, balls of blaze: and they did not pale nor
    pine,
    For earth had attained to heaven, there was no more near nor
    far.

Nay more; for there wanted not who walked in the glare and
    glow,
  Presences plain in the place; or, fresh from the protoplast,
Furnished for ages to come, when a kindlier wind should blow, 35
  Lured now to begin and live, in a house to their liking at last;
Or else the wonderful Dead who have passed through the body
    and gone,
  But were back once more to breathe in an old world worth
    their new:
What never had been, was now; what was, as it shall be anon;
  And what is, – shall I say, matched both? for I was made
    perfect too.   40

All through my keys that gave their sounds to a wish of my soul,
  All through my soul that praised as its wish flowed visibly
    forth,
All through music and me! For think, had I painted the whole,
  Why, there it had stood, to see, nor the process so wonder-
    worth:
Had I written the same, made verse – still, effect proceeds from
    cause,   45
  Ye know why the forms are fair, ye hear how the tale is told;
It is all triumphant art, but art in obedience to laws,
  Painter and poet are proud in the artist-list enrolled: –

But here is the finger of God, a flash of the will that can,
  Existent behind all laws, that made them and, lo, they are! 50
And I know not if, save in this, such gift be allowed to man,
  That out of the three sounds he frame, not a fourth sound, but
    a star.
Consider it well: each tone of our scale in itself is nought;
  It is everywhere in the world – loud, soft, and all is said:
Give it to me to use! I mix it with two in my thought;   55
  And, there! Ye have heard and seen: consider and bow the
    head!

Well, it is gone at last, the palace of music I reared;
  Gone! and the good tears start, the praises that come too slow;
For one is assured at first, one scarce can say that he feared,
  That he even gave it a thought, the gone thing was to go.   60

Never to be again! But many more of the kind
    As good, nay, better perchance: is this your comfort to me?
To me, who must be saved because I cling with my mind
    To the same, same self, same love, same God: aye, what was
        shall be.

Therefore to whom turn I but to Thee, the ineffable Name? 65
    Builder and maker, Thou, of houses not made with hands!
What, have fear of change from Thee who art ever the same?
    Doubt that Thy power can fill the heart that Thy power
        expands?
There shall never be one lost good! What was, shall live as before;
    The evil is null, is nought, is silence implying sound; 70
What was good, shall be good, with, for evil, so much good more;
    On the earth the broken arcs; in the heaven, a perfect round.

All we have willed or hoped or dreamed of good, shall exist;
    Not its semblance, but itself; no beauty, nor good, nor power
Whose voice has gone forth, but each survives for the melodist 75
    When eternity affirms the conception of an hour.
The high that proved too high, the heroic for earth too hard,
    The passion that left the ground to lose itself in the sky,
Are music sent up to God by the lover and the bard;
    Enough that He heard it once: we shall hear it by and by. 80

And what is our failure here but a triumph's evidence
    For the fullness of the days? Have we withered or agonised?
Why else was the pause prolonged but that singing might issue
    thence?
    Why rushed the discords in, but that harmony should be
        prized?
Sorrow is hard to bear, and doubt is slow to clear, 85
    Each sufferer says his say, his scheme of the weal and
        woe:
But God has a few of us whom He whispers in the ear;
    The rest may reason and welcome: 'tis we musicians know.

Well, it is earth with me; silence resumes her reign:
    I will be patient and proud, and soberly acquiesce. 90
Give me the keys. I feel for the common chord again.

Sliding by semitones, till I sink to the minor, – yes,
And I blunt it into the ninth, and I stand on alien ground,
   Surveying a while the heights I rolled from into the deep;
Which, hark, I have dared and done, for my resting-place is
     found,   95
   The C major of this life: so, now I will try to sleep.

MATTHEW ARNOLD

The Voice

    As the kindling glances,
       Queen-like and clear,
    Which the moonlight lances
       From her tranquil sphere
    At the sleepless waters   5
       Of a lonely mere,
On the wild whirling waves, mournfully, mournfully,
       Shiver and die;

    As the tears of sorrow
       Mothers have shed –   10
    Prayers that tomorrow
       Shall in vain be sped
    When the flower they flow for
       Lies frozen and dead –
Fall on the throbbing brow, fall on the burning breast,   15
       Bringing no rest;

    Like bright waves that fall
    With a lifelike motion
On the lifeless margin of the sparkling Ocean:
A wild rose climbing on a mouldering wall –   20
A gush of sunbeams through a ruined hall –
Strains of glad music at a funeral: –
       So sad, and with so wild a start

To this long-sobered heart,
So anxiously and painfully,　　　　　25
So dreamily and doubtfully,
And, oh, with such intolerable change
Of thought, such contrast strange,
O unforgotten Voice, thy whispers come,
Like wanderers from the world's extremity,　　　　　30
Unto their ancient home!

In vain, all, all in vain,
They beat upon mine ear again,
Those melancholy tones so sweet and still.
Those lute-like tones which in the long-distant years　　　　　35
Did steal into mine ear:
Blew such a thrilling summons to my will,
Yet could not shake it;
Drained all the life my full heart had to spill,
Yet could not break it.　　　　　40

COVENTRY PATMORE

Prophets Who Cannot Sing

Ponder, ye Just, the scoffs that frequent go
From forth the foe:
'The holders of the Truth in Verity
Are people of a harsh and stammering tongue!
The hedge-flower hath its song;　　　　　5
Meadow and tree,
Water and wandering cloud
Find Seers who see,
And, with convincing music clear and loud,
Startle the adder deafness of the crowd　　　　　10
By tones, O Love, from thee.
Views of the unveiled heavens alone forth bring
Prophets who cannot sing.

Praise that in chiming numbers will not run;
At least, from David until Dante, none,   15
And none since him.
Fish, and not swim?
They think they somehow should, and so they try
But (haply 'tis they screw the pitch too high)
'Tis still their fates   20
To warble tunes that nails might draw from slates.
Poor Seraphim!
They mean to spoil our sleep, and do, but all their gains
Are curses for their pains!'
  Now who but knows   25
That truth to learn from foes
Is wisdom ripe?
Therefore no longer let us stretch our throats
Till hoarse as frogs
With straining after notes   30
Which but to touch would burst an organ-pipe.
Far better be dumb dogs.

CHRISTINA ROSSETTI

The Peal of Bells

Strike the bells wantonly,
  Tinkle tinkle well;
Bring me wine, bring me flowers,
  Ring the silver bell.
All my lamps burn scented oil,   5
  Hung on laden orange trees,
Whose shadowed foliage is the foil
  To golden lamps and oranges.
Heap my golden plates with fruit,
  Golden fruit, fresh-plucked and ripe;   10
  Strike the bells and breathe the pipe;
Shut out the showers from summer hours –

Silence that complaining lute –
   Shut out thinking, shut out pain,
   From hours that cannot come again.   15

Strike the bell solemnly,
   Ding dong deep:
My friend is passing to his bed,
   Fast asleep;
There's plaited linen round his head,   20
   While foremost go his feet –
His feet that cannot carry him.
My feast's a show, my lights are dim;
   Be still, your music is not sweet, –
There is no music more for him: 25
   His lights are out, his feast is done;
His bowl that sparkled to the brim
Is drained, is broken, cannot hold;
My blood is chill, his blood is cold;
   His death is full, and mine begun.   30

T. E. BROWN

The Organist in Heaven

When Wesley died, the angelic orders,
   To see him at the state,
Pressed so incontinent that the warders
   Forgot to shut the gate.
So I, that hitherto had followed   5
   As one with grief o'ercast,
Where for the doors a space was hollowed,
   Crept in, and heard what passed.
And God said:– 'Seeing thou hast given
   Thy life to my great sounds,   10
Choose thou through all the cirque of heaven
   What most of bliss redounds.'

Then Wesley said:– 'I hear the thunder
   Low growling from thy seat –
Grant me that I may bind it under   15
   The trampling of my feet.'
And Wesley said:– 'See, lightning quivers
   Upon the presence walls –
Lord, give me of it four great rivers,
   To be my manuals.'   20
And then I saw the thunder chidden
   As slave to his desire;
And then I saw the space bestridden
   With four great bands of fire;
And stage by stage, stop stop subtending   25
   Each lever strong and true,
One shape inextricably blending,
   The awful organ grew.
Then certain angels clad the Master
   In very marvellous wise,   30
Till clouds of rose and alabaster
   Concealed him from mine eyes.
And likest to a dove soft brooding,
   The innocent figure ran;
So breathed the breath of his preluding,   35
   And then the fugue began –
Began; but, to his office turning,
   The porter swung his key;
Wherefore, although my heart was yearning,
   I had to go; but he   40
Played on; and, as I downward clomb,
   I heard the mighty bars
Of thunder-gusts, that shook heaven's dome,
And moved the balanced stars.

ALGERNON CHARLES SWINBURNE

A Singing Lesson

Far-fetched and dear-bought, as the proverb rehearses,
Is good, or was held so, for ladies: but nought
In a song can be good if the turn of the verse is
   Far-fetched and dear-bought.

As the turn of a wave it should sound, and the thought   5
Ring smooth, and as light as the spray that disperses
Be the gleam of the words for the garb thereof wrought.

Let the soul in it shine through the sound as it pierces
Men's heart with possession of music unsought;
For the bounties of song are no jealous god's mercies,   10
   Far-fetched and dear-bought.

THOMAS HARDY

The Fiddler

The fiddler knows what's brewing
   To the lilt of his lyric wiles:
The fiddler knows what rueing
   Will come of this night's smiles!

He sees couples join them for dancing,   5
   And afterwards joining for life,
He sees them pay high for their prancing
   By a welter of wedded strife.

He twangs: 'Music hails from the devil,
   Though vaunted to come from heaven,   10

For it makes people do at a revel
What multiplies sins by seven.

'There's many a heart now mangled,
    And waiting its time to go,
Whose tendrils were first entangled   15
    By my sweet viol and bow!'

Afternoon Service at Mellstock (circa 1850)

On afternoons of drowsy calm
    We stood in the panelled pew,
Singing one-voiced a Tate-and-Brady psalm
    To the tune of 'Cambridge New'.

We watched the elms, we watched the rooks,   5
    The clouds upon the breeze,
Between the whiles of glancing at our books,
    And swaying like the trees.

So mindless were those outpourings! –
    Though I am not aware   10
That I have gained by subtle thought on things
    Since we stood psalming there.

The Choirmaster's Burial

He often would ask us
That, when he died,
After playing so many
To their last rest,
If out of us any   5

Should here abide,
And it would not task us,
We would with our lutes
Play over him
By his grave-brim   10
The psalm he liked best –
The one whose sense suits
'Mount Ephraim' –
And perhaps we should seem
To him, in Death's dream,   15
Like the seraphim.

As soon as I knew
That his spirit was gone
I thought this his due,
And spoke thereupon.   20

'I think,' said the vicar,
'A read service quicker
Than viols out-of-doors
In these frosts and hoars.
That old-fashioned way   25
Requires a fine day,
And it seems to me
It had better not be.'

Hence, that afternoon,
Though never knew he   30
That he wish could not be,
To get through it faster
They buried the master
Without any tune.

But 'twas said that, when   35
At the dead of next night
The vicar looked out,
There struck on his ken
Thronged roundabout,
Where the frost was greying   40
The headstoned grass,

A band all in white
Like the saints in church-glass,
Singing and playing
The ancient stave   45
By the choirmaster's grave.

Such the tenor man told
When he had grown old.

On the Tune Called the Old-Hundred-and-Fourth

We never sang together
  Ravenscroft's terse old tune
On Sundays or on weekdays,
In sharp or summer weather,
  At night-time or at noon.   5

Why did we never sing it,
  Why never so incline
On Sundays or on weekdays,
Even when soft wafts would wing it
  From your far floor to mine?   10

Shall we that tune, then, never
  Stand voicing side by side
On Sundays or on weekdays? . . .
Or shall we, when for ever
  In Sheol we abide,   15

Sing it in desolation,
  As we might long have done
On Sundays or on weekdays
With love and exultation
  Before our sands had run?   20

A Musical Incident

When I see the room it hurts me
  As with a pricking blade,
Those women being the memoried reason why my cheer deserts
    me. –
  'Twas thus. One of them played
  To please her friend, not knowing   5
  That friend was speedily growing,
  Behind the player's chair,
  Somnolent, unaware
  Of any music there.

I saw it, and it distressed me,   10
  For I had begun to think
I loved the drowsy listener, when this arose to test me
  And tug me from love's brink.
  'Beautiful!' said she, waking
  As the music ceased. 'Heart-aching!'   15
  Though never a note she'd heard
  To judge of as averred –
  Save that of the very last word.

All would have faded in me,
  But that the sleeper brought   20
News a week thence that her friend was dead. It stirred within
    me
  Sense of injustice wrought
  That dead player's poor intent –
  So heartily, kindly meant –
  As blandly added the sigher: 25
  'How glad I am I was nigh her,
  To hear her last tune!' – 'Liar!'
  I lipped. – This gave love pause,
  And killed it, such as it was.

ROBERT BRIDGES

To Joseph Joachim

Belov'd of all to whom that Muse is dear
Who bid her spirit of rapture from the Greek,
Whereby our art excelleth the antique,
Perfecting formal beauty to the ear;
Thou that hast been in England many a year   5
The interpreter who left us nought to seek,
Making Beethoven's inmost passion speak,
Bringing the soul of great Sebastian near:

Their music liveth ever, and 'tis just
That thou, good Joachim, so high thy skill,   10
Rank (as thou shalt upon the heavenly hill)
Laurel'd with them, for thy ennobling trust
Remember'd, when thy loving hand is still
And every ear that heard thee stopt with dust.

The Psalm

While Northward the hot sun was sinking o'er the trees
as we sat pleasantly talking in the meadow,
the swell of a rich music suddenly on our ears
gush'd thru' the wide-flung doors, where village folk in church
stood to their evening psalm praising God together –   5
and when it came to cloze, paused, and broke forth anew.

A great Huguenot psalm it trod forth on the air
with full slow notes moving as a goddess stepping
through the responsive figures of a stately dance

conscious of beauty and of her fair-flowing array   10
in the severe perfection of an habitual grace,
then stooping to its cloze, paused to dance forth anew;

To unfold its bud of melody everlastingly
fresh as in springtime when, four centuries agone,
it wing'd the souls of martyrs on their way to heav'n   15
chain'd at the barbarous stake, mid the burning faggots
standing with their tongues cut out, all singing in the flames –
O evermore, sweet Psalm, shalt thou break forth anew.

Thou, when in France that self-idolatrous idol reign'd
that starv'd his folk to fatten priests and concubines,   20
thou wast the unconquerable pæan of resolute men
who fell in coward massacre or with Freedom fled
from the palatial horror into far lands away,
and England learnt to voice thy deathless strain anew.

Ah! they endured beyond worst pangs of fire and steel   25
torturings invisible of tenderness and untold;
No Muse may name them, nay, no man will whisper them;
sitting alone he dare not think of them – and wail
of babes and mothers' wail flouted in ribald song.
Draw to thy close, sweet Psalm, pause and break forth anew!   30

Thy minstrels were no more, yet thy triumphing plaint
haunted their homes, as once in deserted house
in Orthes, as 'twas told, the maddened soldiery
burst in and searched, but found nor living man nor maid
only the sound flow'd round them and desisted not   35
but when it wound to cloze, paused, and broke forth anew.

And oft again in some lone valley of the Cevennes
where unabsolvèd crime yet calleth plagues on France
thy heavenly voice would lure the bloodhounds on, astray,
hunting their fancied prey afar in the dark night   40
and with its ghostly music mock'd their oaths and knives.
O evermore great Psalm spring forth! spring forth anew!

WILLIAM ERNEST HENLEY

'The Nightingale Has a Lyre of Gold'

The nightingale has a lyre of gold,
    The lark's is a clarion call,
And the blackbird plays but a boxwood flute,
    But I love him best of all.

For his song is all of the joy of life,
    And we in the mad, spring weather,
We two have listened till he sang
    Our hearts and lips together.

London Voluntaries

I

Grave

St Margaret's bells,
Quiring their innocent, old-world canticles,
Sing in the storied air,
All rosy-and-golden, as with memories
Of woods at evensong, and sands and seas   5
Disconsolate for that the night is nigh.
O, the low, lingering lights! The large last gleam
(Hark! how these brazen choristers cry and call!)
Touching these solemn ancientries, and there,
The silent River ranging tide-mark high   10
And the callow, gray-faced Hospital,
With the strange glimmer and glamour of a dream!
The Sabbath peace is in the slumbrous trees,
And from the wistful, the fast-widowing sky
(Hark! how those plangent comforters call and cry!)   15
Falls as in August plots the roseleaves fall.
The sober Sabbath stir –

Leisurely voices, desultory feet! –
Comes from the dry, dust-coloured street,
Where in their summer frocks the girls go by,   20
And sweethearts lean and loiter and confer,
Just as they did an hundred years ago,
Just as an hundred years to come they will:–
When you and I, Dear Love, lie lost and low,
And sweet-throats none our welkin shall fulfil,   25
Nor any sunset fade serene and slow;
But, being dead, we shall not grieve to die.

Of Antique Dances

Before the town had lost its wits,
And scared the bravery from its beaux,
When money-grubs were merely cits,
And verse was crisp and clear as prose,
Ere Chloe and Strephon came to blows   5
For votes, degrees, and cigarettes,
The world rejoiced to point its toes
In Gigues, Gavottes, and Minuets.

The solemn fiddlers touch their kits;
The tinkling clavichord o'erflows   10
With contrapuntal quirks and hits;
And, with all measure and repose,
Through figures grave as royal shows,
The noble airs and pirouettes,
They move, to rhythms Handel knows,   15
In Gigues, Gavottes, and Minuets.

O Fans and Swords, O Sacques and Mits,
That was the better part you chose!
You know not how those gamesome chits,
Waltz, Polka, and Schottische, arose,   20
Nor how Quadrille – a kind of doze

In time and tune – the dance besets;
You aired your fashion to the close
In Gigues, Gavottes, and Minuets.

Envoy

Muse of the many-twinkling hose,   25
Terpischore, O teach your pets
The charm that shines, the grace that glows
In Gigues, Gavottes, and Minuets.

SIR EDMUND GOSSE

Epithalamium

High in the organ-loft, with lilied hair,
   Love plied the pedals with a snowy foot,
   Pouring forth music like scent of fruit,
And stirring all the incense-laden air;
We knelt before the altar's gold rail, where   5
   The priest stood robed, with chalice and palm-shoot,
   With music-men, who bore citole and lute,
Behind us, and the attendant virgins fair;
And so our red aurora flashed to gold,
   Our dawn to sudden sun, and all the while   10
The high-voiced children trebled clear and cold,
   The censer-boys went singing down the aisle,
And far above, with fingers strong and sure,
Love closed our lives' triumphant overture.

Unheard Music

Men say that, far above our octaves, pierce
   Clear sounds that soar and clamour at heaven's high gate,
   Heard only of bards in vision, and saints that wait
In instant prayer with godly-purgèd ears:
This is that fabled music of the spheres,   5
   Undreamed of by the crowd that, early and late,
   Lift up their voice in joy, grief, hope, or hate,
The diapason of their smiles and tears.
The heart's voice, too, may be so keen and high
   That Love's own ears may watch for it in vain,   10
   Nor part the harmonies of bliss and pain,
Nor hear the soul beneath a long kiss sigh,
Nor feel the caught breath's throbbing anthem die
   When closely-twinèd arms relax again.

Rose Fantasia

Rose, that flushing hues didst borrow
      From my lute,
Pink for joy and pale for sorrow, –
      Now 'tis mute,
Droop thine amber lids, and sleep   5
In a tide of perfume deep,
Till the sap of music creep
      To thy root.

Dream; then die the death of roses
      With no pain,   10
Till the yellowing wreck uncloses
      In the rain.
And the ghost of music springs
On its dim grey moth-like wings

> To my lute's neglected strings   15
> Once again.

ERNEST DOWSON

O Mors! Quam Amara Est Memoria Tua Homini Pacem Habenti In Substantiis Suis

> Exceeding sorrow
>   Consumeth my sad heart!
> Because to-morrow
>   We must depart,
> Now is exceeding sorrow   5
>   All my part!
>
> Give over playing,
>   Cast thy viol away:
> Merely laying
>   Thine head my way: 10
> Prithee, give over playing,
>   Grave or gay.
>
> Be no word spoken;
>   Weep nothing: let a pale
> Silence, unbroken   15
>   Silence prevail!
> Prithee, be no word spoken,
>   Lest I fail!

AUBREY BEARDSLEY

The Three Musicians

Along the path that skirts the wood,
    The three musicians wend their way,
Pleased with their thoughts, each other's mood,
    Franz Himmel's latest roundelay,
The morning's work, a new-found theme, their breakfast and the
    summer day.   5

One's a soprano, lightly frocked
    In cool, white muslin that just shows
Her brown silk stockings gaily clocked,
    Plump arms and elbows tipped with rose,
And frills of petticoats and things, and outlines as the warm wind
    blows.   10

Beside her a slim, gracious boy,
    Hastens to mend her tresses' fall,
And dies her favour to enjoy,
    And dies for *réclame* and recall
At Paris and St Petersburg, Vienna and St James's Hall.   15

The third's a Polish Pianist
    With big engagements everywhere,
A light heart and an iron wrist,
    And shocks and shoals of yellow hair,
And fingers that can trill on sixths and fill beginners with despair.

The three musicians stroll along
    And pluck the ears of ripened corn,
Break into odds and ends of song,
    And mock the woods with Siegfried's horn,
And fill the air with Gluck, and fill the tweeded tourist's soul with
    scorn.   25

The Polish genius lags behind,
   And, with some poppies in his hand,
Picks out the strings and wood and wind
   Of an imaginary band,
Enchanted that for once his men obey his beat and understand. 30

The charming cantatrice reclines
   And rests a moment where she sees
Her château's roof that hotly shines
   Amid the dusky summer trees,
And fans herself, half shuts her eyes, and smoothes the frock
  about her knees.   35

The gracious boy is at her feet,
   And weighs his courage with his chance;
His fears soon melt in noonday heat.
   The tourist gives a furious glance,
Red as his guide-book grows, moves on, and offers up a prayer for
  France.   40

WALTER DE LA MARE

Music

When music sounds, gone is the earth I know,
And all her lovely things even lovelier grow;
Her flowers in vision flame, her forest trees
Lift burdened branches, stilled with ecstasies.

When music sounds, out of the water rise   5
Naiads whose beauty dims my waking eyes,
Rapt in a strange dream burns each enchanted face.
With solemn echoing stirs their dwelling-place.

When music sounds, all that I was I am
Ere to this haunt of brooding dust I came;   10
While from Time's woods break into distant song
The swift-winged hours, as I hasten along.

THOMAS HENNELL

Queen Anne's Musicians

Poor Doctor Blow went out of church
Death-struck ere sermon ended –
With staggering tread he's seen to lurch:
Six ermined quiresmen stand aside,
But he's by none befriended.　　　　　　　　　　5
Lights flicker out at organ-perch;
''Twas time he died ' the people sighed,
'By apoplexy struck, 'tis clear he's done for.'

　　The fiddlers, in a wainscot room,
Strike rounds upon the strings:　　　　　　　10
But quakes the floor, and shiv'ring doom
Upsets their quaverings . . .
Their chorus half-way stuck, no door's to run for.

　　Purcell within stone-vaulted abbey
Played pipes or virginals:　　　　　　　　　　15
The thin-drawn notes re-echoed late
And sounded back from loft and walls.
　　Yet now wax quaint and shabby
As chamber-mated pewter spoons
Old tinkling tunes, which creak and grate.　　20
Fate's left instead of luck: what's candle lit in sun for?

NORMAN NICHOLSON

Song at Night

'Music for a while'
Make audible the smile
   That eyes no longer see;
With crying crayon white
Across the unhearing night   5
   The shape of sighs for me.

Music for a time
Resolve the brawls of rhyme
   That chord within my head;
Sweet as starlight, shine,   10
Illuminate the line,
   Setting the word unsaid.

When Dryden's page is bare,
And silent Purcell's air,
   And mute the singing sky,   15
Then let me pluck one name
And echo clear proclaim
   Not I, my dear, not I.

Notes

Note: biblical quotations are from the Authorised Version.

Anon., early to mid-fourteenth century

Sir Orfeo, ll. 25–38, 269–78. A lay (short romance often containing love and fairy elements) on the story of **Orpheus**, anciently believed to be the founder of poetry and music and able to move creatures, trees and rocks with his art, whose bride, Eurydice, was killed by a snake. He descended to the underworld to get her back, charming Hades, king of Hell, so much with his music that he won from him the promise of her return to the upper world provided that he did not look round to see if she was following; he did, and she was again lost to him. His subsequent life was one of grief and loneliness until he was killed by the Maenads (followers of Bacchus): Ovid, *Metamorphoses*, Books X and XI. **2 glee of harping:** harp music. **3 Siker:** certain. **10 That . . . beforn:** who once sat before Orfeo. **18 gan shill:** resounded. **19 there beth:** were there. **20 teth:** assemble. **23 afine:** to the end.

Sir Thomas Wyatt, c. 1503–42

'Blame not my Lute': originally in Devonshire MS Add 17492. As in many lute songs, the instrument is here associated with love and love melancholy. **2 liketh:** pleases. **13 use:** are accustomed. **18 wreak:** take revenge; vent wrath.

Anon, mid-sixteenth century

Of the Death of Phillips: from *Songs and Sonnets* (also known as *Tottel's Miscellany*) (1557). Possibly a lament for either Robert Phillips, Gentleman of the Chapel under Edward VI, or the lutenist Philip van Wilder (d. 1554), apparently 'Mr Phillips' in court records. **3 gittern:** cithern (kind of wire-strung guitar).

Edmund Spenser, c. 1552–99

The Fairy Queen (1590), II.xii.70–72. The false paradise of the lustful witch Acrasia. **2 mote:** might; **dainty:** discriminating. **3 at once:** together; **ground:** earth. **5 wight:** person. **6 read:** discern. **8 consorted:** combined harmoniously. **10 shrouded:** sheltered. **11 attempered:** blended; **sweet:** sweetly. **12 soft:** softly. **13 respondence:** response; **meet:** fitting. **14 meet:** unite. **16 discrete:** distinct. **27 toys:** games.

John Lyly, c. 1554–1606

Song: from *Midas* (1592), IV.i. **1 Pan's Syrinx:** Pan, the Graeco-Roman god of nature, obtained his characteristic pipes as a result of lusting after Syrinx, who, stopped in her flight from him by a river, prayed to the water deities to save her, which they did by turning her into reeds. Finding his arms full of them, Pan cut them into the Pan pipes so that he would have his beloved always with him (Ovid, *Metamorphoses*, I). **5 gittern: On the Death of Phillips, 3n.** above.

George Chapman, c. 1559–1634

Ovid's Banquet of Sense (1595), ll. 145–225. **6 furious:** divinely inspired. **9 furies:** demons, spirits. **13 numbered:** measured, rhythmical. **14 species:** image presented to the senses. **18 dower:** dowry. **20 tried:** refined. **26 swound:** fainting fit. **32 Rise, stones: Davies, Orchestra, 22–3n.** **33 Cynthian:** Cynthia was the moon goddess, presiding over growth and procreation. **35 quick:** alive, burgeon. **37 man ... world: Cowley, Davideis, 30–1n.** **40 Orphean: Sir Orfeo headnote.** **41 stocks:** blocks. **43 Phoebus:** the sun. **47 hecatombs:** great sacrifices (from Greek *hekatos* = hundred + *bous* = ox; thus also suggesting 'hundreds of notes'). **55 regreet:** greeting. **65 queen of ire:** Pallas Athene, virginal warrior goddess of wisdom. **77 transit:** pass across.

Joshua Sylvester, c. 1563–1618

Variable: from *Spectacles. New-Polished Perspective Spectacles of Especial Use to Discern the World's Vanity . . .* (n.d.) in *The Complete Works of Joshua Sylvester*, ed. A. B. Grosart (1880).

William Shakespeare, 1564–1616

The Merchant of Venice (published 1600): from Act V, scene i. Lorenzo speaks. **6 patens:** circular disks. **7–8 orb . . . sings:** Drummond, Sonnet 8, 7n. and **Milton, At a Solemn Music,** 1, 2nn. **13 Diana:** moon goddess of virginity. **27 Orpheus: Sir Orfeo headnote. 28 stockish:** woodenly stupid. **34 Erebus:** outer darkness; the underworld.

The Sonnets (published 1609): **Sonnet 8. 6 unions:** combinations (as in Herbert's **Easter,** st. 3, below). **14 Thou . . . none:** following the proverbial (originally Pythagorean) idea that one is not a number.

Sonnet 128. 5 jacks: the wooden levers, attached to the back of the keyboard of a virginals or spinet, with a vertical quill on one end which plucks the strings when a key (the **wood** of 1.2) is depressed.

The Tempest (1611; published 1623): from Act I, scene ii. Ferdinand speaks. **4 wrack:** shipwreck; death. **6 passion:** sorrow, suffering.

Thomas Campion, 1567–1620

'When to her Lute Corinna Sings': from *A Book of Airs* (1601).

'Follow your Saint . . .': from *A Book of Airs* (1601). **7 still:** ever.

Song: from *Observations in the Art of English Poesy* (1602). **3 either other:** each the other. **6 concent:** harmony.

Sir John Davies, 1569–1626

Orchestra; or, A Poem of Dancing (1596). stanzas 76–80 (ll. 526–60). **5–7 For . . . been:** Rhea hid the infant Jove (later, king of heaven) on Crete to prevent his father, Saturn, from eating him, and his cries were drowned by the frantic dancing of the Curetes; **timbrels:** tambourines. **10 pomps:** pageants, processions. **15 he:** Orpheus (**Sir Orfeo, headnote** above), whose traditional instrument, either lute or lyre, was often said to have had ten strings. **22–3 So . . . song: Musaeus:** reputed son and disciple of Orpheus; **Amphion:** like Orpheus, reputed founder of the art of music who built the walls of Thebes by moving the stones through the power of his lyre; **Linus:** son of Apollo (the sun god and another reputed inventor of music and poetry), and inventor of songs. **24–5 he . . . tongue:** Hercules, who, in his

Gallic form, was shown drawing people after him with the chains of his
eloquence. **26 Theseus:** turned rural Attica into Athenian civilisation.
29–30 Thracian ... stellified: the constellations Lyra and Hercules.
33 Ganymede: cupbearer to Jove and identified with the constellation
Aquarius, pourer of water and wine. **34 Hebe:** goddess of youth and again
cupbearer to the gods.

A Hymn in Praise of Music: attributed to Davies in *A Poetical Rhapsody*, ed.
Francis Davison (1602). **2 Gordian's knot:** At Gordium, in Asia Minor,
Alexander the Great (born 356 BC) cut the knot which, it was said, would be
loosened only by the conqueror of Asia. **4 Of:** by. **10 rude:** uncouth.
11 fond: foolish(ly). **25 antique:** ancient. **27 To:** in order to; **fell:** fierce,
cruel.

Samuel Rowley, d. 1624

*When You See Me, You Know Me, or, The Famous Chronicle History of
King Henry the Eighth* (1605), ll. 2034–61. **1 Tye:** Dr Christopher Tye (*c.*
1500–73), singer and composer, music tutor to Prince Edward (later
Edward VI). **18 beasts:** Clement Paman, On Christmas Day, 15–21.
20–1 The ... Saul: II Samuel 6; I Samuel 16. **25 And ... dead:** I
Corinthians 15.

Ben Jonson, c. 1572–1637

Echo's Song: from *Cynthia's Revels* (1600–1601), I. ii. **4 division:** descant;
elaborate counterpoint. **11 daffodil:** Narcissus, Echo's beloved, fell in love
with his own reflection, pined away, died, and was turned into a daffodil.

To Alphonso Ferrabosco, on his Book: from *Epigrams* in *Works* (1616).
Title: **Ferrabosco** (c. 1575–1628), son of Alphonso (1543–88) the Italian
composer of madrigals, motets and pieces for lute, who served in the court of
Elizabeth I, was a violist and composer who worked for James I, and
composed music for some of Jonson's masques. His **book** is *Airs: By Alfonso
Ferrabosco* (1609), to which the epigram was originally prefixed. **2 building ... tame:** Sir Orfeo, headnote; Davies, Orchestra, 22–3n. **12–13 eight
... high:** Drumond, Sonnet 8, 7n. In the Ptolemaic system (which still
prevailed) the eighth sphere was that of the fixed stars, the ninth the
primum mobile. One ancient reading of the system had the intervals
between the various planetary spheres and the eighth comprising a

complete octave, or **harmony**: see Heninger (**Cowley**, *Davideis*, **20n.** below), p. 72.

Richard Barnfield, 1574–1627

Sonnet: from *Poems in Diverse Humours* (1598). **5 Dowland**: lutenist, singer and composer John Dowland (1563–1626). **7 Spenser**: Spenser's *Fairy Queen* (see above) was, according the rationale offered in the Letter of the Author's appended to the 1590 text, 'a continued allegory, or dark conceit [riddling imaginative construct]'. **10 Phoebus**: Apollo (**Davies**, *Orchestra*, **22–3n.**).

John Fletcher, 1579–1625

Song: from **King Henry VIII** (written in collaboration with Shakespeare; acted 1613), III. i. **5 as**: as if.

William Drummond of Hawthornden, 1585–1649

Sonnet 8: from *Poems*, Part II (1616). **4 ramage**: song. **5 Sith**: since. **7 spheres**: the concentric spheres, one for each planet, each of which was believed to revolve to a different note. **11 stop**: the pressing of a string to produce notes of a higher pitch than it sounds when 'open'. **14 turtle**: the turtle dove, emblem of marital fidelity even in death.

George Wither, 1588–1667

For a Musician: Hymn 38 from *Hallelujah*, Part III (1641). **10 cunning**: skill. **28 ten-stringed law**: the Ten Commandments (Exodus 20); also the strings on the Orphic lute (**Davies**, *Orchestra*, **15n.** above). **37–40 Teach . . . Saul**: David banishes Saul's evil spirit with his playing in I Samuel 16. See also **Cowley**, *Davideis* I, **41–2n.** below.

Robert Herrick, 1591–1674

All poems from *Hesperides* (1648).
To Music, to Becalm his Fever. **2 numbers**: rhythm.

To Mr Henry Lawes. Title: Henry Lawes (1596–1662), singer and composer, Gentleman of the Chapel Royal. **2 gotire**: guitar. **4 Lanier**:

Nicholas Lanier (1588–1666), composer and painter; Master of the Music to Charles I. **5 Wilson:** John Wilson (1595–1674), composer, singer, lutenist; court musician to Charles I. **6 Apollo: Davies, Orchestra, 22–3n.**

Upon Mr Williams Lawes. Title: William Lawes (1602–45), singer, composer, viol player, Gentleman of the Chapel Royal from 1602, brother of Henry Lawes. **2 cypress:** emblem of mourning. **4 viol:** family of stringed instruments, precursors of the violin family, but different in shape, stringing, shape of bow and method of playing (for example, the treble viol, 'equivalent' of the violin, is played on the lap). **7 Amphion: Davies, Orchestra, 22–3n. 8 Terpander:** historical (as opposed to mythological) founder of Greek music, possibly eighth century BC; **Orpheus: Sir Orfeo, headnote.**

Thomas Carew, c. 1594–1640

Song. Celia Singing: from *Poems* (1640). **11 curious mould:** beautiful body.

George Herbert, 1593–1633

Both poems from *The Temple* (1633).
Easter: ll. 1–18 only. **5 calcined:** consumed; purified (alchemical). **11–12 His . . . day:** Christ's sinews on the cross are like the tautly-tuned gut strings on a lute or viol. **13 Consort:** play together; **heart: see Paman, On Christmas Day, st. 1. 15 three parts:** the essential triad of the common chord (root, third, fifth); **vied:** increased.

William Strode, 1600–43

On a Gentlewoman that Sang and Played Upon a Lute: from *Poetical Works* (1655). **1 music . . . spheres:** William Drummond, Sonnet 8, 7n. above. **7 noise . . . Nile:** presumably referring to the sistrum or metal rattle used in the worship of the Egyptian goddess Isis, who was responsible for Nile fertility.

Owen Feltham, c. 1602–68

Upon a Rare Voice: from *Lusoria: or, Occasional Pieces* as appended to his moral essays *Resolves* (1661). **Title: rare:** seldom found; exceptionally fine. **3 round:** sphere. **6 rests:** remainders (the fragments of sound overflowing

out of heaven from the anthems; the anthems themselves are the product of
the everlasting rest of heaven).

John Milton, 1608–74

Il Penseroso, ll. 131–66: from *Poems of Mr John Milton* (1645). **Title:** 'The
thoughtful' (also 'melancholic') man. **4 Sylvan:** Sylvanus, Roman wood
god. **6 rude:** rough. **7 nymph:** specifically, water deity; here, minor deities
in general. **9 close:** secret. **15 consort:** musical harmony. **21–3 And . . .
good:** compare **Shakespeare, *Tempest*,** excerpt above. **26 pale:** enclosure.
27 embowed: arched. **28 massy:** i.e. made of great stone blocks; **proof:**
impenetrability. **29 storied:** narrating biblical stories; **dight:** ornamented.

At a Solemn Music: from *Poems* (1645). **1 sirens:** one is assigned to each of
the spheres of the cosmos by Plato, *Republic*, X. 616–17. **2 sphere-borne:**
carried on spheres. **4 Dead . . . pierce:** the Orpheus myth (**Sir Orfeo,
headnote** above). **5 fantasy:** imagination, the receiver of images within the
brain. **6 concent:** harmonious accord. **7 sapphire:** Ezekiel 1:26. **9 jubilee:**
year of liberty and restoration, celebrated with the sounds of a trumpet
(Leviticus 25). **10 seraphim:** traditionally **burn** with God's love. **14 With
. . . palms:** Revelation 7:9. **18 noise:** melody; musical band. **20 chime:**
harmonious system. **23 diapason:** the octave, symbol of concordant
relationship in the Christianised version of Pythagorean/Platonic numero-
logy inherited from St Augustine and others: before the Fall (Genesis 3), we
were in perfect accord with God.

Paradise Lost (second edition, 1674), Book I, 531–59. **2 clarions:** shrill,
narrow trumpets used as call to war. **7 meteor:** comet. **8 emblazed:**
splendidly decorated; adorned with heraldic devices. **12 concave:** vault.
13 reign: realm. **16 orient:** bright; barbarically eastern. **20 phalanx:**
square battle formation; **Dorian mood:** the Doric mode was anciently
regarded as inducing courage with self-control (Plato, *Republic*, III. 10).
22 temper: temperament.

Abraham Cowley, 1618–67

Davideis (1656), Book I (lines unnumbered). **2 numbers:** poetic metre; the
numerical basis, in thought-systems derived from Pythagoreanism and
Platonism, underlying the structures of the cosmos and body. **11–16 God's
poem . . . thought:** the analogy between poetic and cosmic creation was a

commonplace: e.g. George Puttenham, *The Art of English Poesy* (1589), I.i. The numerical harmonising of the four warring elements (earth, water, air, fire) was first described in Plato, *Timaeus*, 32 B-C (and see Macrobius, *Commentary on the Dream of Scipio*, I.vi.22–33). The biblical authority for the numerical structure of the universe was the apocryphal Wisdom of Solomon 11:21 ('Thou hast ordered all things in measure, and number, and weight'). **12 rude:** rough, barbaric. **17 tenor:** mean (middle): earth is lowest, water and air are in the middle, fire is the highest element. Earth is therefore the **bass** (lowest voice; foundation or base); the middle elements provide the middle voices (tenor, counter-tenor); fire equates with the treble line. **19 active moon:** because of its swift orbit. **20 Saturn:** the slowest of the planets, hence melancholic and **grave** (solemn; heavy). For images of the cosmos as a stringed instrument (**Saturn's string**), see S. K. Heninger, Jr, *The Cosmographical Glass* (1977), pp. 133, 139. **24 decent:** appropriate; fitting; **dance:** compare **Davies, Orchestra**, above. **27 rehearse:** recite. **30–1 The lesser ... harmony:** man as microcosm, containing within himself the equivalent of the four elements in the shape of the four bodily humours (blood, phlegm, yellow and black bile), was also regarded as being proportioned physically according to the ratios that produce the basic musical intervals ($2:1$ = the octave, etc.; so that if, for example, the distance between base of nose and crown of head is ideally twice that between bottom of chin and base of nose, then they are in octave proportion to each other): see Heninger, *passim*. The idea was formulated by Vitruvius, *Ten Books on Architecture*, III.i. **32 first ... inspire:** God breathed life into Adam (Genesis 2:7); man is therefore in part a wind instrument. **41–2 Thus ... soul: Wither, For a Musician, 37–40n.** above. The effect of music on the passions (due to man's harmonic structure) was affirmed by Plato, *Timaeus*, 47D, and was regarded as the inspiration of the Orpheus myth.

Andrew Marvell, 1621–78

Music's Empire: from *Miscellaneous Poems* (1681). **5 Jubal:** 'the father of all such as handle the harp and organ' (Genesis 4:21); Judaic equivalent of Orpheus. **6 jubilee: Milton, At a Solemn Music, 9n.** above. Marvell suggests a false etymology (jubal-ee). **7 sullen:** gloomy. **9 consort:** mate; also musical harmony. **18 solemn:** sacred. **20 sphere:** heaven. **22 gentler conqueror:** perhaps Lord General Fairfax (former leader of the Parliamentary army, and Marvell's employer for a time), or maybe Oliver Cromwell.

Henry Vaughan, 1621–95

The Morning Watch: from *Silex Scintillans*, Part I (1650). **Title:** early morning prayer. **8 bloods:** makes eager. **10 quick:** living. **15 in . . . kinds:** according to their natures. **16 hurled:** whirled. **17 chime:** Milton, At a Solemn Music, 20n. **18 symphony:** harmony. **23 climb:** through prayer.

Church Service: from *Silex Scintillans*, Part I (1650). **3 dove:** the Holy Spirit. **4–5 Whose . . . moans:** Romans 8:26. **6 dust, stones:** man's sinful, mortal self. **8 stony heart:** as opposed to the spirituality dedicated 'fleshy heart' of 2 Corinthians 3:3. **12 quite:** utterly.

Thomas Stanley, 1625–78

Celia Singing: from *Poems* (1651).

Clement Paman, fl. 1660

On Christmas Day: To my Heart: British Library Add. MS 18220; printed in Alastair Fowler (ed.), *The New Oxford Book of Seventeenth-Century Verse* (Oxford: OUP, 1991). **4 hearts . . . strings:** compare **Herbert, Easter. 6 fall:** of man (Genesis 3). **7 pastoral:** historically the lowest genre of poetry, dealing with shepherds' loves, etc.; but the angels announced Christ's birth first to shepherds (Luke 2). **35 ground:** (1) basis; (2) ground bass (i.e. constant repeated bass motif over which the other parts interweave and vary).

John Dryden, 1631–1700

A Song for St Cecilia's Day, 1687: first edn 1687. **Title:** St Cecilia, third-century Roman martyr, famed as singer and instrumentalist, is the patron saint of music (especially sacred music). Her feast day is 22 November; her symbolic attribute is the organ (see ll. 42–7). For the background to the poem, see **Cowley, *Davideis*** notes, above. **4 jarring:** warring. **6 tuneful voice:** compare the trumpet of judgement at l. 61, and woodcut of God creating the universe from nothing by blowing through a clarion in Heninger (*Davideis*, 20n.), p. 16. **8 cold . . . dry:** the qualities of the four elements. Each element has two of the qualities, which it shares with the other elements thus: fire = hot and dry; air = hot and moist; water = cold and moist; earth = cold and dry. **15 diapason:** Milton, Solemn Music, 23n.;

Cowley, *Davideis*, 30–1n. 16 **passion:** *Davideis*, 41–2n. 17 **Jubal:** Marvell, Music's Empire, 5n. **25–41 The . . . dame:** four stanzas on each of the four temperaments (the temperaments were caused by the humours: *Davideis*, 30–1n.): warlike choleric (yellow bile) with its martial **trumpet** and **drum**; melancholic (black bile), with its **woes**, and **flute** and **lute** (both melancholic instruments in the iconography of the time); phlegmatic (moved by **sharp** instrumental sounds, such as those of the **violin**); and sanguine (blood), the perfect temperament symbolised by the supreme, Cecilian, instrument, the **organ**. 48 **Orpheus:** Sir Orfeo, headnote. 61 **trumpet:** 1 Corinthians 15:52.

An Ode, on the Death of Mr Henry Purcell: first edn 1696. **Title:** Purcell (1659–95), celebrated composer and court musician was organist of Westminster Abbey from 1679 and became one of the three organists of the. Chapel Royal in 1682. 6 **Philomel:** nightingale (Ovid, *Metamorphoses*, 6)). 17 **Orpheus:** Sir Orfeo, headnote. 25 **scale:** Latin *scala* = ladder; and Genesis 28:12 (Jacob's ladder). 32 **mend:** amend; make reparation for.

Samuel Pordage, 1633–c. 1691

To Lucia Playing her Lute: from *Poems upon Several Occasions* (1660). 6 **ela:** highest note of instrumental or vocal compass. Originally, in the gamut or 'great scale' (which comprised all the notes recognised in mediaeval music, and began with G on the bottom line of the bass stave), it was the topmost note, E in the top space of the treble stave.

John Wilmot, second Earl of Rochester (1647–80)

Spoken Extempore to a Country Clerk . . . : from *The Works of the Right Honourable the Earls of Rochester and Roscommon*. 3rd edn (1709). 1 **Sternhold and Hopkins:** *The Whole Book of Psalms*, translated by Thomas Sternhold (d. 1549), John Hopkins (d. 1570) and others was added to the Prayer Book in 1562.

Ambrose Philips, 1674–1749

To Signora Cuzzoni: from *The Musical Miscellany* (1731). **Title: Francesca Cuzzoni** (*c.* 1698–1770), celebrated Italian soprano who sang for Handel in the 1720s. This poem was spawned by the rivalries between champions of Italian and English vernacular opera in the early-middle eighteenth century: see Gay's *Beggar's Opera* (1728) and **Pope, *Dunciad*** and **Miller, Harlequin-Horace** extracts.

Alexander Pope, 1688–1744

The Dunciad, Book IV. 45–68: first published 1743. [P] after a note indicates that it is taken from Pope's own satirical annotations. **1 When . . . by:** 'The attitude given to this phantom represents the nature and genius of Italian opera – its affected airs, its effeminate sounds, and the practice of patching up these operas with favourite songs incoherently put together' [P]. **9 cara, cara:** darlings, darlings. **10 division:** also, musically, an elaborate ornamental run. 'Alluding to the false taste of playing tricks in music with numberless divisions [trills and runs], to the neglect of that harmony which conforms to the sense . . . Mr Handel had introduced a great number of hands, and more variety of instruments into the orchestra, and employed even drums and cannon to make a fuller chorus'[P]. **16 encore:** a new, affected, 'un-English' habit. **17 Phoebus:** god of the sun and harmony. **21 Handel:** George Frideric (1685–1759), celebrated German-born organist and composer and main force behind the vogue for Italian *opera seria*. **22 Briareus:** mythological 100-handed giant who, with other giants, battled against Jove and was buried by him under Etna.

John Byrom, 1692–1763

Epigram on Handel and Bononcini: published in *Swift and Pope: Miscellanies in Verse and Prose* (1727–35); text from Byrom, *Poems* (1773), vol. I. **Title: Handel:** Pope, *Dunciad*, 21n.; Giovanni Maria **Bononcini** (1642–78) lived and died in Modena; composer of operas, cantatas, etc. **2 Mynheer:** Mr (Dutch; but Dutch and Deutsch [German] were interchangeable in the xenophobic satire of the time). **6 Tweedle-dum and Tweedle-dee:** the first use of the phrase, based on **tweedle** = to play an instrument shrilly + **de-dum-de-dum**.

Henrietta Knight, Lady Luxborough, 1699–1756

The Bullfinch in Town: from Robert Dodsley (ed.), *A Collection of Poems by Several Hands*, 6 vols. (1748–58), vol. IV. The habit of training birds to sing opera tunes, etc. was common at the time: see, for example, *The Bird Fancier's Delight* (1717), which opens with tunes for the bullfinch.

James Miller, 1706–44

Harlequin-Horace (1731) (lines unnumbered).
11 beaux: fashionable young men. 12 nose: syphilis, known as the Italian disease, eats into the nose cartilage. 14 vizard: mask (as worn in the currently fashionable masquerades (l. 17)). 15 South Sea schemes: investors made and lost vast amounts of money in the South Sea Company, the market in whose shares collapsed in 1720. 18 Heidegger: John James Heidegger (c. 1659–1749), Swiss-born promoter of masquerades and other entertainments in London; collaborated with Handel in producing operas in the 1720s-30s. 21 Gallic horn: French horn, new in the early eighteenth century. 22 fiddle: from the mid-seventeenth century the violin began to displace the treble viol; flute: the native recorder (English flute) was displaced by the transverse (German) flute in the mid-eighteenth century. 24 bassoon: another new instrument in the 1720s. 26 Roman capon: castrati filled main soprano parts in contemporary Italian opera (e.g. Francesco Senesino, Carlo Farinelli); strum: the action of playing unmusically; harlot. 29 Dullness: the heroine of Pope's Dunciad. 30 gamut: scale (see also Pordage, To Lucia, 6n.).

Samuel Johnson, 1709–84

An Epitaph upon the Celebrated Claudy Philips: from the Gentleman's Magazine (September, 1740). Title: Charles Claudius Philips, violinist, died 1732.

Christopher Smart, 1722–71

Jubilate Agno [Rejoice in the Lamb], Fragment B, ll. 582–597: written 1758–63, first printed in edition by W. F. Stead (1939), re-edited W. F. Bond (1954) from the autograph MS in Houghton Library, Harvard University. Text from Jubilate Agno, ed. Karina Williamson (Oxford: Clarendon Press, 1980). This section is based on the idea of the music of creation (as in Cowley, Davideis, above) and particularly creation as an organ (Heninger as at Davideis, 20n., p. 24). 2 thunder-stop: e.g. 1 Samuel 7:10. 5 shawm: early oboe. 11 Baumgarden: bassonist in London theatre orchestras from late 1750s.

Anna Seward, 1747–1809

Epitaph for John Saville (editor's title): memorial on the west wall of the

south transept of Lichfield Cathedral, where **Saville** (*c.* 1735–1803) was a
counter-tenor vicar-choral. The actual heading to the epitaph is 'Sacred to
the Memory of John Saville, 48 years vicar-choral of this Cathedral. Ob:
Aug'sta. 2ndo 1803 Aeta 67'. Also printed in Peter Giles, *The History and
Technique of the Counter-tenor* (Aldershot, Hampshire: Scolar Press, 1994).
4 gratulating: felicitating; joyful.

William Blake, 1757–1827

Song: from *An Island in the Moon*, (1784), ch. 11.

William Lisle Bowles, 1762–1850

At Ostend: from *Sonnets* (1789).

William Wordsworth, 1770–1850

On the Power of Sound, ll. 129–208: from *Yarrow Revisited and Other Poems*
(1835). **1 Amphion:** Davies, Orchestra, 22–3n. **3 Arion:** lyric poet who,
while sailing from his native Lesbos to Italy, was attacked and robbed by the
crew. Granted his request to play the harp before he was killed, he played so
sweetly that he attracted a dolphin. He leaped onto its back and it carried
him safely to Tenedos; it was rewarded by being made into a constellation.
17 Pan: John Lyly, Song, 1n. **19–20 leopards . . . vines:** leopards traditionally drew the chariot of Bacchus, god of wine. **23 Silenus:** Bacchus's
drunken companion and servant. **38 songstress:** Philomel, the nightingale, reputedly sings of her rape by Tereus (and see **Dryden, An Ode, on . . .
Henry Purcell, 6n.**). **75 six-days' work:** the creation, according to Genesis
1; **flaming seraphim:** Milton, At a Solemn Music, 10n. **78 mood:** musical
mode. **79 gratulation:** rejoicing.

The Solitary Reaper: from *Poems in Two Volumes* (1807).

Sonnet: Inside of King's College, Cambridge: from *Poems in Five Volumes*,
3rd edn (1827). **1 royal saint:** King Henry VI (reigned 1422–61; murdered
1471), traditionally regarded as holy or a saint, founded King's College,
Cambridge, and Eton College, in 1441.

The Same: *ibid.* **1 awful:** awe-inspiring. **7 prison bars:** the lead canes
retaining the stained glass of the portraits. **5 eremite:** hermit.

Samuel Taylor Coleridge, 1772–1834

Ode on the Ottery and Tiverton Church Music: from *Poems on Various Subjects* (1796). Coleridge was the youngest son of the vicar of Ottery St Mary, Devon. **3 sphere-descended:** Milton, Solemn Music, 2n. **8 Legion:** e.g. Mark 5 (the man Legion possessed by devils which depart into swine).

The Aeolian Harp: first published in *Poems on Various Subjects* (1796); this version, in *Sibylline Leaves* (1817). **Title:** the **Aeolian** (or wind) **harp** consisted of a wooden box just about a metre long strung with catgut strings of various thicknesses. Although tuned in unison, the strings sounded different harmonics (according to the thickness of the string) when the harp was placed by an open window, etc. **1 Sara:** Coleridge's wife, *née* Fricker. **45 framed:** formed, contrived. **47 Plastic:** creative, shaping.

On a Volunteer Singer: from *Poetical Works* (1828).

Lines Composed in a Concert Room: *ibid.* **19 tedded:** scattered about for drying.

George Gordon, Lord Byron, 1788–1824

'The Harp the Monarch Minstrel Swept': from *Hebrew Melodies* (1815). **Title:** the poem is about David, the 'cunning player on an harp' of 1 Samuel 16:16.

Percy Bysshe Shelley, 1792–1822

To —: from *Posthumous Poems*, ed. Mary Shelley (1824).

Lines: 'When the Lamp is Shattered': *ibid.*

With a Guitar, to Jane: from *The Athenaeum*, 20 October 1832. **Title: Jane:** i.e. Jane Williams, whom Shelley got to know in Italy in 1820.

Thomas Lovell Beddoes, 1803–49

Hymn: from *Poems* (1851).

Alfred, Lord Tennyson, 1809–92

Song: from *Poems by Two Brothers* (1827).

The Dying Swan: from *Poems, Chiefly Lyrical* (1830). **18 marish:** marsh. **26 coronach:** funeral lament. **32 shawms: Smart, Jubilate Agno, 5n.**

'The Splendour Falls on Castle Walls': from *The Princess* (1847): 3rd edn (revised) (1850); lyric inserted between sections III and IV.

Orlando Gibbons: from a letter to C. V. Stanford dated 1 June 1885 in the possession of the Royal College of Music, London; printed in Christopher Ricks (ed.), *The Poems of Tennyson*, 2nd edn (Longman: Harlow, 1987), III. 639. **Title: Gibbons** (1583–1625), composer and organist, was organist of the Chapel Royal from 1604, and at Westminster Abbey from 1623.

William Bell Scott, 1811–90

Music: from *A Poet's Harvest Home* (1882). **29 Dead March of Saul:** popular name for the well-known funeral march from Handel's oratorio *Saul* (1739).

Robert Browning, 1812–89

Abt Vogler: from *Dramatis Personae* (1864). **Title: Georg Joseph Vogler** (Abbé Vogler) (1749–1814), composer, theorist, organist, and founder of music schools. Taught Browning's music teacher, John Relfe. Celebrated for his pyrotechnics at the keyboard; invented a 'simplification system' for the organ. **1 brave:** splendid. **3 Solomon:** the wise biblical king was tradition-ally believed to have controlled spirits through his mystical five-pointed seal. **8 princess:** Pharaoh's daughter (1 Kings 7:8). **23 Rome's dome:** St Peter's, illuminated on certain special occasions. **34 protoplast:** the first creator; or the first created thing. **93 ninth:** the discordant chord of the ninth (for example, if the root note is G, the chord consists of the root, the third above it (B), and the fifth (D), seventh (F), and ninth (A)) was a favourite of Vogler's. **96 C major:** the simplest chord and key, containing no sharps or flats.

Matthew Arnold, 1822–88

The Voice: from *The Strayed Reveller, and Other Poems* (1849).

Coventry Patmore, 1823–96

Prophets Who Cannot Sing: from Book II of *To the Unknown Eros* (1877).
15 David: the biblical king and psalmist; **Dante:** Dante Alighieri
(1265–1321), author of the *Divina Commedia* (*Divine Comedy*).

Christina Rossetti, 1830–94

The Peal of Bells: from *Goblin Market and Other Poems* (1862).

T[homas] E[dward] Brown, 1830–97

The Organist in Heaven: from *Collected Poems of T. E. Brown*, ed. H. F.
Brown *et al.* (1900). **2 state:** the divine throne. **13 Wesley:** Samuel
Sebastian Wesley (1810–76), organist and composer, and almost single-
handedly responsible for raising the standard of Anglican church music
through his superb anthems, etc. Among other positions, he was organist of
Hereford (1832–5), Exeter (1835–41), Winchester (1849–65) and Glou-
cester (1865–76) Cathedrals. **16 The ... feet:** i.e. through the organ
pedals. **19–20 Lord ... manuals:** the four rivers of paradise (Genesis 2)
become the four keyboards. **28 awful:** awe-inspiring.

Algernon Charles Swinburne, 1837–1909

A Singing Lesson: from *A Century of Roundels* (1883).

Thomas Hardy, 1840–1928

The Fiddler: from *Time's Laughing Stocks* (1909). **16 viol: Robert Herrick,
Upon William Lawes, 4n.**

Afternoon Service at Mellstock (*circa* 1850): from *Moments of Vision*
(1917). **3 Tate-and-Brady:** Nahum Tate (d. 1715) and Nicholas Brady (d.
1726) collaborated in a metrical version of the Psalms that, published in
1696 and authorised by William III, was printed in the Prayer Book
alongside the standard Authorised Bible translation. **4 'Cambridge New':**
psalms are sung to any metrically suitable hymn melody. I have been
unable to trace this hymn; Hardy may have invented the name.

The Choirmaster's Burial: from *Moments of Vision* (1917). **13 'Mount
Ephraim':** hymn tune by Benjamin Milgrove (1731–1810). **8 lutes:**

church bands used whatever instruments were available (compare **viols**, l. 23); organs, along with robed choirs, belonged to the later nineteenth century, as parish churches began to emulate the cathedrals. **45 ancient stave:** i.e. the eighteenth-century tune, as written down musically on its five-line staff.

On the Tune Called the Old-Hundred-and-Fourth: from *Late Lyrics and Earlier* (1922). **Title:** the tune from Thomas Ravenscroft's *Psalter* (1621), set to Psalm 104 and still occasionally in use under the title 'Old 104th'. **15 Sheol:** the underworld; the grave.

A Musical Incident: from *Winter Words* (1928).

Robert Bridges, 1844–1930

To Joseph Joachim: from the *Monthly Review*, June 1904. **Title: Joachim** (1831–1907), Hungarian violin virtuoso, celebrated for his interpretation of Beethoven's Violin Concerto (l. 7) and the dedicatee and first performer of Brahms's Violin Concerto. **8 Sebastian:** the celebrated German composer and organist Johann Sebastian Bach (1685–1750).

The Psalm: from *New Verse* (1925). **7 Huguenot:** this name for French protestants emerged from the religious wars that broke out in France in the sixteenth century. The main background to the poem is the Massacre of St Bartholomew's Day, 24 August, 1572, when between 20,000 and 100,000 Huguenot men, women and children were slaughtered on the orders of Charles IX and his mother, Catherine de' Medici. **24 England:** religious toleration was granted to Huguenots in 1681, which led to a considerable influx of emigrés escaping persecution under Louis XIV.

William Ernest Henley, 1849–1903

'The Nightingale Has a Lyre of Gold': *Echoes*, XVIII, from *Poems* (1921). **3 boxwood:** a common, and excellent, wood for wind instruments.

London Voluntaries: published 1893. **Tempo mark:** *Grave:* solemnly. **1 St Margaret's:** St Margaret's, Westminster. **2 canticles:** here, the sung parts of Evensong.

Of Antique Dances: from *Bric-à-Brac* in *Poems* (1921). **5 Chloe, Strephon:** type names for girl and boy in pastoral love poetry of the late seventeenth and early eighteenth centuries. **8 Gigues:** (or jigs): lively dances in 6/8 (or 9/8 or 12/8) time; **Gavottes:** French seventeenth-century dances, lively, in common time, and starting on the third beat of the bar; **Minuets:** dance in triple time, adopted into seventeenth-century society from French rustic dance. **9 kits:** dancing masters' pocket fiddles. **15 Handel: Pope,** *Dunciad*, **21n. 17 Sacque:** loose gown worn by ladies; also, in eighteenth century, long silk train attached to gown; **Mit:** i.e. mitt, or fingerless lace glove which stretches up forearm. **20 Polka:** quick dance in duple time, introduced from Bohemia in 1830s; **Schottische:** literally, Scottish [dance]: polka-like dance of foreign origin introduced into England in 1848. **21 Quadrille:** square dance, introduced into England from France in late eighteenth century. **26 Terpischore:** Muse of dancing.

Sir Edmund Gosse, 1849–1928

Epithalamium: from *On Viol and Flute* (1873). **Title:** marriage song. **7 citole:** mediaeval stringed instrument of guitar type.

Unheard Music: from *Sonnets and Quatorzains* in *Collected Poems* (1911). **8 diapason:** octave.

Rose Fantasia: from *Songs of Roses* in *Collected Poems* (1911).

Ernest Dowson, 1867–1900

O Mors! Quam Amara Est . . .: from *Verses* (1896). **Title:** 'O Death, how bitter is your memory to a man at peace among his goods' (Ecclesiasticus 41:1, Vulgate Bible).

Aubrey Beardsley, 1872–98

The Three Musicians: from *The Savoy*, January 1896. **4 Franz Himmel:** perhaps recalling the opera and operetta composer Friedrich Himmel (1765–1814). **8 clocked:** embroidered with a circular (clock-like) motif. **14 réclame:** publicity. **24 Siegfried:** eponymous hero of the third opera of Wagner's *Der Ring des Nibelungen* (1876). **25 Gluck:** the German opera composer Christoph Willibald von Gluck (1714–87).

Walter de la Mare, 1873–1956

Music: from *Motley and Other Poems* (1917). **6 Naiads:** water deities. **12 hours:** also: goddesses of the seasons.

Thomas Hennell, 1903–45

Queen Anne's Musicians: from *Poems* (London: Oxford University Press, 1936). **Title: Queen Anne** reigned 1702–14. **1 Doctor Blow:** Dr John Blow (1649–1708), composer, and organist of Westminster Abbey from 1668–79, when he was succeeded by his pupil Henry **Purcell** (l. 14, and see **Dryden, An Ode, on the Death of Mr Henry Purcell** above), and again from 1695–1708.

Norman Nicholson, 1914–87

Song at Night: published in *Rock Face* (1948); text from Neil Curry (ed.), *Collected Poems* (London: Faber, 1994). **1 'Music for a while':** aria for alto or tenor from Purcell's music for Dryden's *Oedipus* (1692).

Acknowledgements

The editor and publishers wish to thank the following for permission to use copyright material:

Miss Elizabeth Hennell for Thomas Hennell, 'Queen Anne's Musicians' from *Poems*, Oxford University Press (1936); David Higham Associates on behalf of the author for Norman Nicholson, 'Song at Night' from *Rock Face*, Faber and Faber; The Society of Authors as the representative of the Literary Trustees of the author for Walter de la Mare, 'Music' from *The Complete Poems of Walter de la Mare*, 1969.

Every effort has been made to trace the copyright holders but if any have been inadvertently overlooked the publishers will be pleased to make the necessary arrangement at the first opportunity.